GUJARAT

A STATE STUDY GUIDE

P. K. SHAH

HAWK PRESS

Published by

Hawk Press
4836/24, Ansari Road, Daryaganj
New Delhi – 110 002
Phones: 91-11-23278618, 91-11-43667199
E-mail: thehawkpress@gmail.com
www.thehawkpress.com

Preface

Gujarat state is one of the developed states in India with its fourth rank in per capita income among the major states. The economy of the state has done particularly well in the 1990s by taking good advantage of the new opportunities created by the economic reforms. The enterprising population, with the support of the state government, has accessed new opportunities to raise the rate of growth to one of the highest in the country. However, these achievements are also accompanied by several weak points such as, almost stagnant agricultural growth, massive degradation and depletion of natural resources, heavy pollution in several industrial and urban centres, relatively low achievements in human development and wide regional disparities.

The state of Gujarat is thus very rich in archaeological heritage and the present book attempts to document this aspect in a concise form. The book consists of a brief history of Gujarat from the Stone Age to the British rule, important monuments and archaeological sites and their importance and exhaustive list of sites from lower Paleolithic to the British times. This is basically a reference book useful to all those interested in the subject.

The Gujaratis have a long historical and cultural tradition dating back to the days of the Harappan civilization established by relics found at Lothal. Situated on the western part of the Indian sub-continent, Gujarat derives its name 'Gujaratta' meaning the land of Gurjars. The Gurjars passed through the Punjab and settled in some parts of Western India, which came to be known as Gujarat.

Agriculture in Gujarat forms a vital sector of the state's

economy. It provides the required food grains for the state's population and raw materials for most of the agro-based industries. There was a development of industries like Chemicals, petrochemicals, fertilizers, engineering, electronics etc. With the largest Petro-chemical complex in the country, Gujarat is a major producer of inorganic chemicals such as soda-ash and caustic soda as well as chemical fertilizers.

The three important languages of Gujarat are Gujarati, Urdu and Sindhi. There are eleven variants or dialects of Gujarati. The majority of the people of Gujarat speak Gujarati which belongs to the Indo-Aryan family. This language is derived from Sanskrit and other ancient languages. It was also highly influenced by Apabrahmsa, which was widely spoken in the north west India from the 10th to 14th centuries. The maritime contact with Persia, Arabia, Portugal and England further led to the introduction of many words from these languages. Kachchi as a mother tongue was spoken in Kutch.

The state is the world's largest producer of processed diamonds, accounting for 72 per cent of the world's processed diamond share and 80 per cent of India's diamond exports. With a contribution of 65 to 70 per cent to India's denim production, Gujarat is the largest manufacturer of denim in the country and the third largest in the world. There are 42 ports, 18 domestic airports and one international airport. There are 106 product clusters and 60 notified special economic zones (SEZs). Large scale investment is expected in Gujarat as part of the US$ 90 billion Delhi-Mumbai Industrial Corridor (DMIC).

This is a reference book. All the matter is just compiled and edited in nature, taken from the various sources which are in public domain.

The present book examines the different dimensions of the dynamics of development of Gujarat in order to understand the processes and to infer policy interventions for a healthy and sustainable development.

—Editor

ABOUT THE BOOK

Gujarat state is one of the developed states in India with its fourth rank in per capita income among the major states. The economy of the state has done particularly well in the 1990s by taking good advantage of the new opportunities created by the economic reforms. The enterprising population, with the support of the state government, has accessed new opportunities to raise the rate of growth to one of the highest in the country. However, these achievements are also accompanied by several weak points such as, almost stagnant agricultural growth, massive degradation and depletion of natural resources, heavy pollution in several industrial and urban centres, relatively low achievements in human development and wide regional disparities. Gandhinagar is the capital of the state, while Ahmedabad is the largest city in it. The state held its present form in the year 1960 when the Bombay state was divided into Maharashtra and Gujarat on the basis of language. Ever since its inception, the state of Gujarat has maintained its momentum of growth. With just 5 per cent of India's total population and 6 per cent of geographical area, the state of Gujarat contributes 16 per cent of country's total investment, 10 per cent of expenditure, 16 per cent of exports and 30 per cent of stock market capitalization. Such an economic performance, development initiatives, infrastructure, programmes and schemes and dynamic leadership have placed the state in leading position. The present book examines the different dimensions of the dynamics of development of Gujarat in order to understand the processes and to infer policy interventions for a healthy and sustainable development.

Contents

1

State at a Glance

Gujarat is a state in Western India and Northwest India with an area of 196,024 km(75,685 sq mi), a coastline of 1,600 km (990 mi) – most of which lies on the Kathiawar peninsula – and a population in excess of 60 million. It is the sixth largest Indian state by area and the ninth largest state by population. Gujarat is bordered by Rajasthan to the northeast, Daman and Diu to the south, Dadra and Nagar Haveli and Maharashtra to the southeast, Madhya Pradesh to the east, and the Arabian Sea and the Pakistani province of Sindh to the west.

Its capital city is Gandhinagar, while its largest city is Ahmedabad. The Gujarati-speaking people of India are indigenous to the state. The economy of Gujarat is the third-largest state economy in India with 14.96 lakh crore (US$210 billion) in gross domestic product and a per capita GDP of 157,000(US$2,200).

The state encompasses some sites of the ancient Indus Valley Civilisation, such as Lothal, Dholavira, and Gola Dhoro. Lothal is believed to be one of the world's first seaports. Gujarat's coastal cities, chiefly Bharuch and Khambhat, served as ports and trading centers in the Maurya and Gupta empires, and during the succession of royal Saka dynasties from the Western Satraps era. Along with Bihar and Nagaland, Gujarat is one of the three Indian states to prohibit the sale of alcohol.

ETYMOLOGY

Present-day Gujarat is derived from Sanskrit term *Gurjaradesa*, meaning the land of the Gurjaras who ruled Gujarat in the 8th and 9th centuries CE. Parts of modern Rajasthan and Gujarat have been known as *Gurjaratra* or *Gurjarabhumi* (land of the Gurjars) for centuries before the Mughal period.

HISTORY

Ancient history

Dholavira, one of the largest cities of Indus Valley Civilisation, with stepwell steps to reach the water level in artificially constructed reservoirs.

Gujarat was one of the main central areas of the Indus Valley Civilisation. It contains ancient metropolitan cities from the Indus Valley such as Lothal, Dholavira, and Gola Dhoro. The ancient city of Lothal was where India's first port was established. The ancient city of Dholavira is one of the largest and most prominent archaeological sites in India, belonging to the Indus Valley Civilisation. The most recent discovery was Gola Dhoro.

Altogether, about 50 Indus Valley settlement ruins have been discovered in Gujarat.

Archaeological remains of washroom drainage system at Lothal.

The ancient history of Gujarat was enriched by the commercial activities of its inhabitants. There is clear historical evidence of trade and commerce ties with Egypt, Bahrain and Sumer in the Persian Gulf during the time period of 1000 to 750 BC. There was a succession of Hindu and Buddhist states such as the Mauryan Dynasty, Western Satraps, Satavahana dynasty, Gupta Empire, Chalukya dynasty, Rashtrakuta Empire, Pala Empireand Gurjara-Pratihara Empire, as well as local dynasties such as the Maitrakas and then the Chaulukyas.

The early history of Gujarat reflects the imperial grandeur of Chandragupta Maurya who conquered a number of earlier states in what is now Gujarat. Pushyagupta, a Vaishya, was appointed the governor of Saurashtra by the Mauryan regime. He ruled Giringer (modern day Junagadh) (322 BC to 294 BC) and built a dam on the Sudarshan lake. Emperor Ashoka, the grandson of Chandragupta Maurya, not only ordered engraving of his edicts on the rock at Junagadh but asked Governor Tusherpha to cut canals from the lake where an earlier Mauryan governor had built a dam. Between the decline of Mauryan power and Saurashtra coming under the sway of the Samprati Mauryas of Ujjain, there was an Indo-Greek defeat in Gujarat of Demetrius. In 16th century manuscripts, there is an apocryphal story of a merchant of King Gondaphares landing in Gujarat with Apostle Thomas. The incident of the cup-bearer torn apart by a lion might indicate that the port city described is in Gujarat.

For nearly 300 years from the start of the 1st century AD, Saka rulers played a prominent part in Gujarat's history. The weather-beaten rock at Junagadh gives a glimpse of the ruler Rudradaman I (100 AD) of the Saka satraps known as Western Satraps, or Kshatraps. Mahakshatrap Rudradaman I founded the Kardamaka dynasty which ruled from Anupa on the banks of the Narmada up to the Aparanta region which bordered Punjab. In Gujarat, several battles were fought between the south Indian Satavahana dynasty and the Western Satraps. The greatest and the mightiest ruler of the Satavahana Dynasty was Gautamiputra Satakarni who defeated the Western Satraps and conquered some parts of Gujarat in the 2nd century CE.

Coin of the Gujuras of Sindh, Chavda dynasty, circa 570–712 CE. Crowned Sasanian-style bust right / Fire altar with ribbons and attendants; star and crescent flanking flames.

The Kshatrapa dynasty was replaced by the Gupta Empire with the conquest of Gujarat by Chandragupta Vikramaditya. Vikramaditya's successor Skandagupta left an inscription (450 AD) on a rock at Junagadh which gives details of the governor's repairs to the embankment surrounding Sudarshan lake after it was damaged by floods. The Anarta and Saurashtra regions were both parts of the Gupta empire. Towards the middle of the 5th century, the Gupta empire went into decline. Senapati Bhatarka, the Maitraka general of the Guptas, took advantage of the situation and in 470 AD he set up what came to be known as the Maitraka state. He shifted his capital from Giringer to Valabhipur, near Bhavnagar, on Saurashtra's east coast. The Maitrakas of Vallabhi became very powerful with their rule prevailing over large parts of Gujarat and adjoining Malwa. A university was set up by the Maitrakas, which came to be known far and wide for its scholastic pursuits and was compared with the noted Nalanda University. It was during the rule of Dhruvasena Maitrak that Chinese philosopher-traveler Xuanzang/ I Tsingvisited in 640 AD along the Silk Road.

Gujarat was known to the ancient Greeks and was familiar with other Western centers of civilization through the end of the European Middle Ages. The oldest written record of Gujarat's 2,000-year maritime history is documented in a Greek book titled *The Periplus of the Erythraean Sea: Travel and Trade in the Indian Ocean by a Merchant of the First Century.*

Medieval history

Sun Temple of Modhera, with stepwell surrounding the Kunda (tank), was built by Bhima I of Chaulukya dynasty in 1026 CE. It is one of the finest examples of stepwell architecture of Gujarat.

Rani ki vav 11th century CE.

Taranga Jain Temple constructed by Kumarapala(1143–1172 CE).

In the early 8th century, the Arabs of the Umayyad Caliphate established an Empire in the name of the rising religion Islam, which stretched from Spain in the west to Afghanistan and modern-day Pakistan in the east. Al-Junaid, the successor of Qasim, finally subdued the Hindu resistance within Sindh and had established a secure base. The Arab rulers tried to expand their empire southeast, which culminated in the Caliphate campaigns in India fought in 730 CE. However, the Arab invaders were defeated and repelled from the areas east of the Indus river, probably by a Hindu alliance between Nagabhata I of the Pratihara Dynasty, Vikramaditya II of the Chalukya dynasty and Bappa Rawal of Guhila dynasty. After this victory, the Arab invaders were driven out of Gujarat. General Pulakeshin, a Chalukya prince of Lata, received the title *Avanijanashraya* (refuge of the people of the earth) and honorific of "Repeller of the unrepellable" by the Chalukya emperor Vikramaditya II for his victory at the battle at Navsari, where the Arab troops suffered a crushing defeat.

In the late 8th century, the Kannauj Triangle period started. The three major Indian dynasties – the northwest Indian Gurjara-Pratihara Dynasty, the south Indian Rashtrakuta Dynasty and the east Indian Pala Empire – dominated India from the 8th to 10th centuries. During this period the northern part of Gujarat was ruled by the north Indian Gurjara-Pratihara dynasty and the southern part of Gujarat was ruled by the south Indian Rashtrakuta dynasty. However, the earliest epigraphical records of the Gurjars of Broach attest that the royal bloodline of the Gurjara-Pratihara dynasty of Dadda I-II-III (650–750) ruled south Gujarat. Southern Gujarat was ruled by the south Indian Rashtrakuta dynasty until it was captured by the south Indian ruler Tailapa II of the Western Chalukya Empire.

Zoroastrians from Greater Iran migrated to the western borders of South Asia (Gujarat and Sindh) during the 8th or 10th century, to avoid persecution by Muslim invaders who were in the process of conquering Iran. The descendants of those Zoroastrian refugees came to be known as the Parsi.

Subsequently, in southern Gujarat was ruled by the Rashtrakuta dynasty until it was captured by the Western Chalukya ruler Tailapa II.

The Chaulukya dynasty ruled Gujarat from c. 960 to 1243. Gujarat was a major center of Indian Ocean trade, and their capital at Anhilwara (Patan) was one of the largest cities in India, with population estimated at 100,000 in the year 1000. After 1243, the Solankis lost control of Gujarat to their feudatories, of whom the Vaghela chiefs of Dholka came to dominate Gujarat. In 1292 the Vaghelas became tributaries of the Yadava dynasty of Devagiri in the Deccan. Karandev of the Vaghela dynasty was the last Hindu ruler of Gujarat. He was defeated and overthrown by the superior forces of Alauddin Khalji from Delhi in 1297. With his defeat, Gujarat not only became part of the Muslim empire but the Rajput hold over Gujarat lost for ever.

According to Barnes (2017), fragments of printed cottons made in Gujarat, India were discovered in Egypt, which provides evidence for medieval trade in the western Indian Ocean. These fragments represent the Indian cotton traded to Egypt during the Fatimid, Ayyubid and Mamluk periods from tenth to sixteenth centuries. Similar Gujarati cottons were traded as far east as Indonesia, and this is contextualized under the medieval trades of the wider Indian Ocean.

MUSLIM RULE

Islamic Conquests 1197–1614 AD

After the Ghoris had assumed a position of Muslim supremacy over North India, Qutbuddin Aibak attempted to conquer Gujarat and annex it to his empire in 1197 but failed in his ambitions. An independent Muslim community continued to flourish in Gujarat for the next hundred years, championed by Arab merchants settling along the western coast belonging to the Shafi'ite madhhab. From 1297 to 1300, Allauddin Khilji, the Turkic Sultan of Delhi, destroyed the Hindu metropolis of Anhilwara and incorporated Gujarat into the Delhi Sultanate. After Timur's sacking of Delhi at the end of the 14th century weakened the Sultanate, Gujarat's Muslim Rajput governor Zafar Khan Muzaffar (Muzaffar Shah I) asserted his independence, and his son, Sultan Ahmed Shah (ruled 1411 to 1442), established Ahmedabad as the capital. Khambhat eclipsed Bharuch as Gujarat's most important trade port. Gujarat's relations with Egypt, which was then the premier Arab power in the Middle East remained friendly over the next century and the Egyptian scholar, *Badruddin-ad-Damamimi*, spent several years in Gujarat in the shade of the Sultan before proceeding to the Bahmani Sultanate of the Deccan.

Shah e Alam, a famous Sufi-saint of the Chishti order who was the descendant of Makhdoom Jahaniyan Jahangasht from Bukhara soon arrived among other luminaries such as Arab theologian *Ibn Suwaid*, several Sayyid Sufi members of the Aydarus family of Tarim in Yemen, Iberian court interpreter *Ali al-Andalusi* from Granada, and the Arab jurist *Bahraq* from Hadramaut who was appointed a tutor of the prince. Among the illustrious names who arrived during the reign of Mahmud Begada was the philosopher *Haibatullah Shah Mir* from Shiraz, and the scholar intellectual *Abu Fazl Ghazaruni* from Persia who tutored and adopted Abu'l-Fazl ibn Mubarak, author of the *Akbarnama*. Later, a close alliance between the Ottoman Turks and Gujarati sultans to effectively safeguard Jeddah and the Red Sea trade from Portuguese imperialism, encouraged the existence of powerful Rumi elites within the kingdom who took the post of viziers in Gujarat keen to maintain ties with the Ottoman state.

Humayun had also briefly occupied the province in 1536, but fled due to the threat Bahadur Shah, the Gujarat king, imposed. The Sultanate of Gujarat remained independent until 1572, when the Mughal emperor Akbar the Great conquered it and annexed it to the Mughal Empire.

The Surat port (the only Indian port facing westwards) then became the principal port of India during Mughal rule to gain widespread international repute. The eminent city of Surat, famous for its cargo export of silk and diamonds had come on a par with contemporary Venice and Beijing which were some of the great mercantile cities of Europe and Asia, and earned the distinguished title, *Bab al-Makkah* (Gate of Mecca).

Drawn by the religious renaissance taking place under Akbar, Mohammed Ghaus moved to Gujarat and established spiritual centers for the Shattari Sufi order from Iran, founding the Ek Toda Mosque and producing such devotees as Wajihuddin Alvi of Ahmedabad whose many successors moved to Bijapur during the height of the Adil Shahi dynasty. At the same time, Zoroastrian high priest Azar Kayvan who was a native of Fars, immigrated to Gujarat founding the Zoroastrian school of illuminationists which attracted key Shi'ite Muslim admirers of the Safavid philosophical revival from Isfahan.

Early 14th-century Maghrebi adventurer, Ibn Batuta, who famously visited India with his entourage, recalls in his memoirs about Cambay, one of the great emporia of the Indian Ocean that indeed:

Cambay is one of the most beautiful cities as regards the artistic architecture of its houses and the construction of its mosques. The reason is that the majority of its inhabitants are foreign merchants, who continually build their beautiful houses and wonderful mosques – an achievement in which they endeavor to surpass each other.

Many of these "foreign merchants" were transient visitors, men of South Arabian and Persian Gulf ports, who migrated in and out of Cambay with the rhythm of the monsoons. But others were men with Arab or Persian patronyms whose families had settled in the town generations, even centuries earlier, intermarrying with Gujarati women, and assimilating everyday customs of the Hindu hinterland.

The Age of Discovery heralded the dawn of pioneer Portuguese and Spanish long-distance travel in search of alternative trade routes to "the East Indies", moved by the trade of gold, silver and spices. In 1497, Portuguese explorer Vasco da Gama is said to have discovered the Europe-to-India sea route which changed the course of history, thanks to Kutchisailor Kanji Malam, who showed him the route from the East African coasts of Mozambique sailing onwards to Calicut off the Malabar coast in India. Later, the Gujarat Sultanate allied with the Ottomans and Egyptian Mamluks naval fleets led by governor-generals Malik Ayyaz and Amir Husain Al-Kurdi, vanquished the Portuguese in the 1508 Battle of Chaul resulting in the first Portuguese defeat at sea in the Indian Ocean.

To 16th-century European observers, Gujarat was a fabulously wealthy country. The customs revenue of Gujarat alone in the early 1570s was nearly three times the total revenue of the whole Portuguese empire in Asia in 1586–87, when it was at its height. Indeed, when the British arrived on the coast of Gujarat, houses in Surat already had windows of Venetian glass imported from Constantinople through the Ottoman empire. In 1514, the Portuguese explorer Duarte Barbosa described the cosmopolitan atmosphere of Randerknown otherwise as *City of Mosques* in Surat province, which gained the fame and reputation of illustrious Islamic scholars, Sufi-saints, merchants and intellectuals from all over the world:

Ranel (Rander) is a good town of the Moors, built of very pretty houses and squares. It is a rich and agreeable place ... the Moors of the town trade with Malacca, Bengal, Tawasery (Tannasserim), Pegu, Martaban, and Sumatra in all sort of spices, drugs, silks, musk, benzoin and porcelain. They possess very large and fine ships and those who wish Chinese articles will find them there very completely. The Moors of this place are white and well dressed and very rich they have pretty wives, and in the furniture of these houses have china vases of many kinds, kept in glass cupboards well arranged. Their women are not secluded like other Moors, but go about the city in the day time, attending to their business with their faces uncovered as in other parts.

The conquest of the Kingdom of Gujarat marked a significant event of Akbar's reign. Being the major trade gateway and departure harbour of pilgrim ships to Mecca, it gave the Mughal Empire free access to the Arabian sea and control over the rich commerce that passed through its ports. The territory and income of the empire were vastly increased.

The Sultanate of Gujarat and the merchants

A modern ZoroastrianAgiary in Western India

For the best part of two centuries, the independent Rajput Sultanate of Gujarat was the cynosure of its neighbors on account of its wealth and prosperity, which had long made the Gujarati merchant a familiar figure in the ports of the Indian Ocean. Gujaratis, including Hindus and Muslims as well as the enterprising Parsi class of Zoroastrians, had been specializing in the organisation of overseas trade for many centuries, and had moved into various branches of commerce such as commodity trade, brokerage, money-changing, money-lending and banking.

By the 17th century, Chavuse and Baghdadi Jews had assimilated into the social world of the Surat province, later on their descendants would give rise to the Sassoons of Bombay the Ezras of Calcutta, and other influential Indian-Jewish figures who went on to play a philanthropical role in the commercial development of 19th-century British Crown Colony of Shanghai. Spearheaded by Khoja, Bohra, Bhatiya shahbandars and Moorish nakhudas who dominated sea navigation and shipping, Gujarat's transactions with the outside world had created the legacy of an international transoceanic empire which had a vast commercial network of permanent agents stationed at all the great port cities across the Indian Ocean. These networks extended to the Philippines in the east, East Africa in the west, and via maritime and the inland caravan route to Russia in the north.

As Tome Pires, a Portuguese official at Malacca, writing of conditions during the reigns of Mahmud I and Mozaffar II, expressed it: "Cambay stretches out two arms; with her right arm she reaches toward Aden and with the other towards Malacca" (Pires, I, p. 41) and also described Gujarat's active trade with Goa, Deccan and the Malabar. His contemporary, Duarte Barbosa, describing Gujarat's maritime trade, recorded the import of horses from the Middle East and elephants from Malabar, and lists exports which included *muslins, chintzes* and *silks, carnelian, ginger* and *other spices, aromatics, opium, indigo* and *other substances for dyeing, cereals* and *legumes* (Barbosa, I, pp. 108–58). Persia was the destination for many of these commodities, and they were partly paid for in horses and pearlstaken from Hormuz (Barbosa, I, p. 82). It was the latter item, in particular, which led Sultan Sikandar Lodi of Delhi, according to Ali-Muhammad Khan, author of the Mirat-i-Ahmadi, to complain that the *"support of the throne of Delhi is wheat and barley but the foundation of the realm of Gujarat is coral and pearls"* (apud Bayley, p. 20). Hence, the sultans of Gujarat possessed ample means to sustain lavish patronage of religion and the arts, to build madrasas and kanaqahs, and to provide douceurs for the literati, mainly poets and historians, whose presence and praise enhanced the fame of the dynasty.

Even at the time of Tom Pires' travel to the East Indies in the early 16th century, Gujarati merchants had earned an international reputation for their commercial acumen and this encouraged the visit of merchants from Cairo, Armenia, Abyssinia, Khorasan, Shiraz, Turkestan and Guilans from Aden and Hormuz. Pires noted in his *Suma Orientale*:

These [people] are [like] Italians in their knowledge of and dealings in merchandise ... they are men who understand merchandise; they are so properly steeped in the sound and harmony of it, that the *Gujaratees* say that any offence connected with merchandise is pardonable. There are *Gujaratees* settled everywhere. They work some for some and others for others. They are diligent, quick men in trade. They do their accounts with fingers like ours and with our very writings.

Gujarat in the Mughal Empire

Gujarat was one of the twelve original subahs (imperial top-level provinces) established by Mughal padshah (emperor) Akbar the Great, with seat at Ahmedabad, bordering on Thatta (Sindh), Ajmer, Malwa and later Ahmadnagar subahs.

Aurangzeb, who was better known by his imperial title Alamgir ("Conqueror of the World"), was born at Dahod, Gujarat, and was the sixth Mughal Emperor ruling with an iron fist over most of the Indian subcontinent. He was the third son and sixth child of Shah Jahan and Mumtaz Mahal. At the time of his birth, his father, Shah Jahan, was then the Subahdar (governor) of Gujarat, and his grandfather, Jehangir, was the Mughal Emperor. Before he became emperor, Aurangzeb was made Subahdar of Gujarat subah as part of his training and was stationed at Ahmedabad. Aurangzeb was a notable expansionist and was amongst the wealthiest of the Mughal rulers, with an annual yearly tribute of £38,624,680 (in 1690). During his lifetime, victories in the south expanded the Mughal Empire to more than 3.2 million square kilometers and he ruled over a population estimated as being in the range of 100–150 million subjects.

Aurangzeb had great love for his place of birth. In 1704, he wrote a letter to his eldest son, Muhammad Azam Shah, asking him to be kind and considerate to the people of Dahod as it was his birthplace. Muhammad Azam was then the Subedar (governor) of Gujarat.

In his letter, Aurangzeb wrote:

My son of exalted rank, the town of Dahod, one of the dependencies of Gujarat, is the birthplace of this sinner. Please consider a regard for the inhabitants of that town as incumbent on you.

Maratha Empire

When the cracks had started to develop in the edifice of the Mughal empire in the mid-17th century, the Marathas were consolidating their power in the west, Chatrapati Shivaji, the great Maratha ruler, attacked Surat in southern Gujarat twice first in 1664 and again in 1672. These attacks marked the entry of the Marathas into Gujarat. However, before the Maratha inroads into Gujarat, the Europeans had made their presence felt, with the Portuguese leading them, followed by the Dutch and the English.

The Peshwas had established their sovereignty over parts of Gujarat and collected taxes and tributes through their representatives. Damaji Gaekwad and Kadam Bande divided the Peshwa's territory between them, with Damaji establishing the sway of Gaekwad over Gujarat and made Baroda(present day Vadodara in southern Gujarat) his capital. The ensuing internecine war among the Marathas was fully exploited by the British, who interfered in the affairs of both Gaekwads and the Peshwas.

In Saurashtra, as elsewhere, the Marathas were met with resistance. The decline of the Mughal Empire helped form larger peripheral states in Saurashtra, including Junagadh, Jamnagar, Bhavnagar and a few others, which largely resisted the Maratha incursions.

European Colonialism 1614–1947 AD

In the 1600s, the Dutch, French, English and Portuguese all established bases along the western coast of the region. Portugal was the first European power to arrive in Gujarat, and after the Battle of Diu, acquired several enclaves along the Gujarati coast, including Daman and Diuas well as Dadra and Nagar Haveli. These enclaves were administered by Portuguese India under a single union territory for over 450 years, only to be later incorporated into the Republic of India on 19 December 1961 by military conquest.

The British East India Company established a factory in Surat in 1614 following the commercial treaty made with Mughal Emperor Nuruddin Salim Jahangir, which formed their first base in India, but it was eclipsed by Bombay after the English received it from Portugal in 1668 as part of the marriage treaty of Charles II of England and Catherine of Braganza, daughter of King John IV of Portugal. The state was an early point of contact with the west, and the first British commercial outpost in India was in Gujarat.

17th-century French explorer François Pyrard de Laval, who is remembered for his 10-year sojourn in South Asia, bears witness accounts that the Gujaratis were always prepared to learn workmanship from the Portuguese, also in turn imparting skills to the Portuguese:

I have never seen men of wit so fine and polished as are these Indians: they have nothing barbarous or savage about them, as we are apt to suppose. They are unwilling indeed to adopt the manners and customs of the *Portuguese*; yet do they regularly learn their manufactures and workmanship, being all very curious and desirous of learning. In fact the *Portuguese* take and learn more from them than they from the *Portuguese*.

Later in the 17th century, Gujarat came under control of the Hindu Maratha Empire that rose defeating the Muslim Mughals and who dominated the politics of India. Most notably, from 1705 to 1716, Senapati Khanderao Dabhade led the

Maratha Empire forces in Baroda. Pilaji Gaekwad, first ruler of Gaekwad dynasty, established the control over Baroda and other parts of Gujarat.

The British East India Company wrested control of much of Gujarat from the Marathas during the Second Anglo-Maratha War in 1802–1803. Many local rulers, notably the Rajput Maratha Gaekwad Maharajas of Baroda (Vadodara), made a separate peace with the British and acknowledged British sovereignty in return for retaining local self-rule.

An epidemic outbreak in 1812 killed half the population of Gujarat.

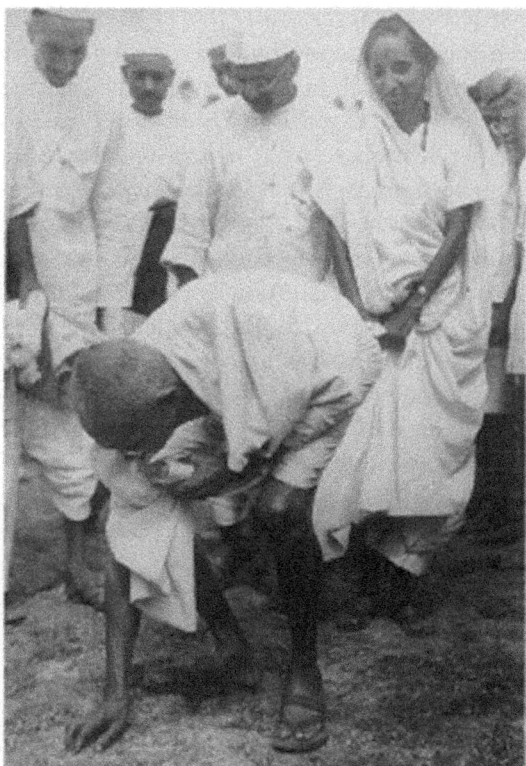

Mahatma Gandhi picking salt at Dandi beach, South Gujarat ending the Salt satyagraha on 5 April 1930

Gujarat was placed under the political authority of the Bombay Presidency, with the exception of Baroda state, which had a direct relationship with the Governor-General of India. From 1818 to 1947, most of present-day Gujarat, including Kathiawar, Kutch and northern and eastern Gujarat were divided into hundreds of princely states, but several districts in central and southern Gujarat, namely Ahmedabad, Broach (Bharuch), Kaira (Kheda), Panchmahal and Surat, were governed directly by British officials.

Post independence

After Indian independence and the partition of India in 1947, the new Indian government grouped the former princely states of Gujarat into three larger units; Saurashtra, which included the former princely states on the Kathiawad peninsula, Kutch, and Bombay state, which included the former British districts of Bombay Presidency together with most of Baroda state and the other former princely states of eastern Gujarat. Bombay state was enlarged to include Kutch, Saurashtra (Kathiawar) and parts of Hyderabad state and Madhya Pradesh in central India. The new state had a mostly Gujarati-speaking north and a Marathi-speaking south. Agitation by Gujarati nationalists, the Mahagujarat Movement, and Marathi nationalists, the Samyukta Maharashtra, for their own states led to the split of Bombay state on linguistic lines; on 1 May 1960, it became the new states of Gujarat and Maharashtra. In 1969 riots, at least 660 died and properties worth millions were destroyed.

The first capital of Gujarat was Ahmedabad; the capital was moved to Gandhinagar in 1970. *Nav Nirman Andolan* was a socio-political movement of 1974. It was a students' and middle-class people's movement against economic crisis and corruption in public life. This was the first and last successful agitation after the Independence of India that ousted an elected government.

The Morvi dam failure, in 1979, resulted in the death of thousands of people and large economic loss. In the 1980s, a reservation policy was introduced in the country, which led to anti-reservation protests in 1981 and 1985. The protests witnessed violent clashes between people belonging to various castes.

The 2001 Gujarat earthquake was located about 9 km south-southwest of the village of Chobari in Bhachau Taluka of Kutch District. This magnitude 7.7 shock killed around 20,000 people (including at least 18 in South-eastern Pakistan), injured another 167,000 and destroyed nearly 400,000 homes.

In February 2002, the Godhra train burning lead to statewide riots, resulting in the deaths of 1044 people – 790 Muslims and 254 Hindus, and hundreds missing still unaccounted for. Akshardham Temple was attacked by two terrorists in September 2002, killing 32 people and injuring more than 80 others. National Security Guards intervented to end siege killing both terrorists. On 26 July 2008 a series of seventeen bomb blasts rocked the city, killing and injuring several people.

LANGUAGE

Languages of Gujarat (2011)

Gujarati (85.97%)

Hindi (7.06%)

Sindhi (1.96%)

Marathi (1.52%)

Urdu (0.79%)

Others (2.7%)

Gujarati is an Indo-Aryan language evolved from Sanskrit and local Prakrits, and is part of the greater Indo-Europeanlanguage family. It is native to the Indian state of Gujarat, and is its main language, as well as of the adjacent union territories of Daman and Diu and Dadra and Nagar Haveli.

About 49 million people speak Gujarati, making it the 26th most-spoken native language in the world. Along with Romani, Kutchi, and Sindhi, it is amongst the most western of Indo-Aryan languages. According to the 52nd report of the commissioner for linguistic minorities under Ministry of Minority Affairs, majority of the population speak Gujarati with 84.40% speakers, followed by Bhili (4.75%), Hindi (4.71%), Sindhi (1.89%), Marathi (1.51%) and Urdu (1.09%).

People from the Kutch region of Gujarat also speak in the Kutchi mother tongue, and to a great extent appreciate Sindhi as well. Memoni is the mother tongue of Kathiawar and Sindhi Memons, most of them who are exclusively Muslims.

Almost 88% of the Gujarati Muslims speak Gujarati as their mother tongue, whilst the other 12% speak Urdu. A sizeable proportion of Gujarati Muslims are bilingual in both languages; Islamic academic institutions (Darul Uloom) place a high prestige on learning Urdu and Arabic, with students' memorising the Quran and *ahadith*, and emphasising the oral and literary importance of mastering these languages as a compulsory rite of religion. Other native languages spoken in low proportions are Bhili and Gamit, which are spoken exclusively among the tribals. Apart from this, English, Marwari, Sindhi, Punjabi, Tamil, Kannada, Telugu, Bengali, Odia, Malayalam, Marathi and others are spoken by a considerable number of economic migrants who have flocked to the state in recent decades seeking employment and higher standards of living.

The languages taught in schools under the three-language formula are: First Language: Gujarati/Hindi/Marathi/English/ Urdu Second Language: Gujarati/English Third Language: Hindi. In previous years, Sindhi was also taught as a first language, but this has changed.

ECONOMY

During the British Raj, Gujarati businesses served to play a major role to enrich the economy of Karachi and Mumbai. Major agricultural produce of the state includes cotton, groundnuts (peanuts), dates, sugar cane, milk and milk products. Industrial products include cement and petrol. According to a 2009 report on economic freedom by the Cato Institute, Gujarat is the first most free state in India (the second one being Tamil Nadu). Reliance Industries operates the oil refinery at Jamnagar, which is the world's largest grass-roots refinery at a single location. The world's largest shipbreaking yard is in Gujarat near Bhavnagar at Alang. India's only Liquid Chemical

Port Terminal at Dahej, developed by Gujarat Chemical Port
Terminal Co Ltd. Gujarat has two of the three liquefied natural
gas (LNG) terminals in the country (Dahej and Hazira). Two
more LNG terminals are proposed, at Pipavav and Mundra.

Mundra Port Kutch

Gujrat has 85% village connectivity with allweather roads.
Nearly 100% of Gujarat's 18,000 villages have been connected
to the electrical grid for 24-hour power to households and eight
hours of power to farms, through the Jyotigram Yojana. As of
2015, Gujarat ranks first nationwide in gas-based thermal
electricity generation with a national market share of over 8%,
and second nationwide in nuclear electricity generation with
national market share of over 1%. More than 900,000 internet
users and all villages are connected with broadband internet.
The state registered 12.8% agricultural growth in the last five
years against the national average of 2%.

Gujarat records highest decadal agricultural growth rate of
10.97%. Over 20% of the *S&P CNX 500* conglomerates have
corporate offices in Gujarat. As per RBI report, in year 2006–07,
26% out of total bank finance in India was in Gujarat.

In a July 2011 report, The Economist referred to Gujarat as India's Guangdong. As per a recent survey report of the Chandigarh Labour Bureau, Gujarat has the lowest unemployment rate of 1% against the national average of 3.8%.

It also has the biggest industrial area for ceramic business in Morbi, Himatanagar, which produces around 80% of the country's gross ceramic production and around 80% of compact fluorescent lamp (CFL). Legatum Institute's Global Prosperity Index 2012 has recognised Gujarat as the highest-scoring amongst all states of India on matters of social capital. The state ranks 15th alongside Germany in a list of 142 nations worldwide, and actually ranks higher than several developed nations.

Infrastructure

Tallest Building in Gujarat: GIFT One

Tallest tower in Gujarat, GIFT One was inaugurated on 10 January 2013. One other tower called GIFT Two has been finished and more towers are planned.

Industrial growth

Gujarat's major cities include Ahmedabad, Surat, Vadodara, Rajkot, Jamnagar and Bhavnagar. In 2010, *Forbes* list of the world's fastest growing cities included Ahmedabad at number 3 after Chengdu and Chongqing from China. The state is rich in calcite, gypsum, manganese, lignite, bauxite, limestone, agate, feldspar, and quartz sand, and successful mining of these minerals is done in their specified areas. Jamnagar is the hub for manufacturing brass parts. Gujarat produces about 98% of India's required amount of soda ash, and gives the country about 78% of the national requirement of salt. It is one of India's most prosperous states, having a per-capita GDP significantly above India's average. Kalol, Khambhat, and Ankleshwar are today known for their oil and natural gas production. Dhuvaran has a thermal power station, which uses coal, oil, and gas. Also, on the Gulf of Khambhat, 50 kilometres (31 mi) southeast of Bhavnagar, is the Alang Ship Recycling Yard (the world's largest). General Motors manufactures its cars at Halol near Vadodara, Tata Motors manufactures the Tata Nanofrom Sanand near Ahmedabad, and AMW trucks are made near Bhuj. Surat, a city by the Gulf of Khambhat, is a hub of the global diamond trade. In 2003, 92% of the world's diamonds were cut and polished in Surat. The diamond industry employs 500,000 people in Gujarat.

Petroleum, Chemical and Petrochemical Investment Region (PCPIR) spread across 453,000 square hectares—in Bharuch.

Gujarat is one of the first few states in India to have encouraged private-sector investment, some of which are already in operation. In addition, the liquid cargo (chemicals) handling port at Dahej is also set up in joint sector and made operational. At an investor's summit entitled "Vibrant Gujarat Global Investor Summit", arranged between 11 and 13 January 2015, at Mahatma Mandir, Gandhinagar, the state government signed 21000 Memoranda of Understanding for Special Economic Zones worth a total of 2.5 million crores (short scale). However, most of the investment was from domestic industry. In the fourth

Vibrant Gujarat Global Investors' Summit held at Science City, Ahmedabad, in January 2009, there were 600 foreign delegates. In all, 8668 MOUs worth 12500 billion were signed, estimated to create 2.5 million new job opportunities in the state. In 2011, Vibrant Gujarat Global Investors' Summit MOUs worth 21 trillion (US$ 463 billion) were signed.

Gujarat is state with surplus electricity. The Kakrapar Atomic Power Station(KAPS) is a nuclear power station run by NPCIL that lies in the proximity of the city of Surat. Recently, the Gujarat Government has upgraded its installed capacity of 13,258 megawatts (MW) by adding another 3,488 MW. According to the official sources, against demand of 40,793 million units during the nine months since April 2010, Gujarat produced 43,848 million units. Gujarat sold surplus power to 12 states: Rajasthan, Tamil Nadu, Uttar Pradesh, Maharashtra, Andhra Pradesh, Delhi, Haryana, Karnataka, Chhattisgarh, Uttarakhand, Madhya Pradesh, and West Bengal.

Energy

Astonfield's 11.5 MW solar plant in Gujarat

Gujarat invests in development of solar energy in the state and has had India's largest solar power plant as of January

2012. It has allotted 716 MW of solar power capacity to 34 national and international solar project developers in 2009, against the planned 500 MW capacity under its solar power policy. This is expected to bring in investments of INR 120 billion and generate employment for 5,000 people. By 2014, Gujarat plans on producing 1000MW of energy by solar power.

AGRICULTURE

Traditional farming

The total geographical area of Gujarat is 19,602,400 hectares, of which crops take up 10,630,700 hectares. The three main sources of growth in Gujarat's agriculture are from cotton production, the rapid growth of high-value foods such as livestock, fruits and vegetables, and from wheat production, which saw an annual average growth rate of 28% between 2000 and 2008 (According to the International Food Policy Research Institute). Other major produce includes bajra, groundnut, cotton, rice, maize, wheat, mustard, sesame, pigeon pea, green gram, sugarcane, mango, banana, sapota, lime, guava, tomato, potato, onion, cumin, garlic, isabgul and fennel. Whilst, in recent times, Gujarat has seen a high average annual growth of 9% in the agricultural sector, the rest of India has an annual growth rate of around 3%. This success was lauded by former President of India, Dr. APJ Abdul Kalam.

The strengths of Gujarat's agricultural success have been attributed to diversified crops and cropping patters; climatic diversity (8 climatic zones for agriculture); the existence of 4 agricultural universities in the state, which promote research in agricultural efficiency and sustainability; co-operatives; adoption of hi-tech agriculture such as tissue culture, green houses and shed-net houses; agriculture export zones; strong marketing infrastructure, which includes cold storages, processing units, logistic hubs and consultancy facilities.

Gujarat is the main producer of tobacco, cotton, and groundnuts in India. Other major food crops produced are rice, wheat, *jowar, bajra*, maize, *tur*, and *gram*. The state has an agricultural economy; the total crop area amounts to more than one-half of the total land area.

Animal husbandry and dairying have played vital roles in the rural economy of Gujarat. Dairy farming, primarily concerned with milk production, functions on a co-operative basis and has more than a million members. Gujarat is the largest producer of milk in India. The Amulmilk co-operative federation is well known all over India, and it is Asia's biggest dairy. Amongst livestock raised are buffalo and other cattle, sheep, and goats. As per the results of livestock census 1997, there were 20.97 million head of livestock in Gujarat State. In the estimates of the survey of major livestock products, during the year 2002–03, the Gujarat produced 6.09 million tonnes of milk, 385 million eggs and 2.71 million kg of wool. Gujarat also contributes inputs to the textiles, oil, and soap industries, amongst others.

The adoption of cooperatives in Gujarat is widely attributed to much of the success in the agricultural sector, particularly sugar and dairy cooperatives. Cooperative farming has been a component of India's strategy for agricultural development since

1951. Whilst the success of these was mixed throughout the country, their positive impact on the states of Maharashtra and Gujarat have been the most significant. In 1995 alone, the two states had more registered co-operatives than any other region in the country. Out of these, the agricultural cooperatives have received much attention. Many have focused on subsidies and credit to farmers and rather than collective gathering, they have focused on facilitating collective processing and marketing of produce. However, whilst they have led to increased productivity, their effect on equity in the region has been questioned, because membership in agricultural co-operatives has tended to favour landowners whilst limiting the entry of landless agricultural labourers. An example of co-operative success in Gujarat can be illustrated through dairy co-operatives, with the particular example of Amul (Anand Milk Union Limited).

Amul Plant at Anand

Amul Was formed as a dairy cooperative in 1946, in the city of Anand, Gujarat. The cooperative, Gujarat Co-operative Milk Marketing Federation Ltd. (GCMMF), is jointly owned by around 2.6 million milk producers in Gujarat. Amul has been seen as one of the best examples of cooperative achievement and success in a developing economy and The Amul pattern of growth has been taken as a model for rural development, particularly in the agricultural sector of developing economies. The company stirred the White Revolution of India (also known as Operation Flood), the world's biggest dairy development program, and made the milk-deficient nation of India the largest milk producer in the world, in 2010. The "Amul Model" aims to stop the exploitation by middlemen and encourage freedom of movement since the farmers are in control of procurement, processing and packaging of the milk and milk products. The company is worth 2.5 billion US dollars (as of 2012).

70% of Gujarat's area is classified as semi-arid to arid climatically, thus the demand on water from various economic activities puts a strain on the supply. Of the total gross irrigated area, 16–17% is irrigated by government-owned canals and 83–84% by privately owned tube wells and other wells extracting groundwater, which is the predominant source of irrigation and water supply to the agricultural areas. As a result, Gujarat has faced problems with groundwater depletion, especially after demand for water went up in the 1960s. As access to electricity in rural areas increased, subermersible electric pumps became more popular in the 1980s and 1990s. However, the Gujarat Electricity Board switched to flat tariff rates linked to the horsepower of pumps, which increased tubewell irrigation again and decreased the use of electric pumps. By the 1990s, groundwater abstraction rates exceeded groundwater recharge rate in many districts, whilst only 37.5% of all districts has "safe" recharge rates. Groundwater maintenance and preventing unnecessary loss of the available water supplies is now an issue faced by the state. The Sardar Sarovar Project, a debated dam project in the Narmada valley consisting of a network of canals, has significantly increased irrigation in the region. However, its impact on communities who were displaced is still a contested issue. Recently, in 2012, Gujarat began an experiment to reduce water loss due to evaporation in canals and to increase sustainability in the area by constructing solar panels over the canals. A one megawatt (MW) solar power project set up at Chandrasan, Gujarat uses solar panels fixed over a 750-metre stretch of an irrigation canal. Unlike many solar power projects, this one does not take up large amounts of land since the panels are constructed over the canals, and not on additional land. This results in lower upfront costs since land does not need to be acquired, cleared or modified to set up the panels. The Chandrasan project is projected to save 9 million litres of water per year.

The Government of Gujarat, to improve soil management and introduce farmers to new technology, started on a project which involved giving every farmer a Soil Health Card. This acts like a ration card, providing permanent identification for the status of cultivated land, as well as farmers' names, account numbers, survey numbers, soil fertility status and general fertiliser dose. Samples of land from each village are taken and analysed by the Gujarat Narmada Valley Fertiliser Corporation, State Fertiliser Corporation and Indian Farmers Fertilisers Co-operative. 1,200,000 soil test data from the villages was collected as of 2008, from farmer's field villages have gone into a database. Assistance and advice for this project was given by local agricultural universities and crop and soil-specific data was added to the database. This allows the soil test data to be interpreted and recommendations or adjustments made in terms of fertiliser requirements, which are also added to the database.

CULTURE

Gujarat is home to the Gujarati people. It was also the home of Mahatma Gandhi, a worldwide figure for peaceful struggle against tyranny, and Vallabhbhai Patel, a founding father of the republic of India.

LITERATURE

Gujarati literature's history may be traced to 1000 AD. Well known laureates of Gujarati literature are Hemchandracharya, Narsinh Mehta, Mirabai, Akho, Premanand Bhatt, Shamal Bhatt, Dayaram, Dalpatram, Narmad, Govardhanram Tripathi, Mahatma Gandhi, K. M. Munshi, Umashankar Joshi, Suresh Joshi, Swaminarayan, Pannalal Patel and Rajendra Shah.

Kavi Kant, Zaverchand Meghani and Kalapi are famous Gujarati poets.

Gujarat Vidhya Sabha, Gujarat Sahitya Sabha, and Gujarati Sahitya Parishad are Ahmedabad based literary institutions promoting the spread of Gujarati literature. Saraswatichandrais a landmark novel by Govardhanram Tripathi. Writers like Aanand Shankar Dhruv, Ashvini Bhatt, Balwantray Thakore, Bhaven Kachhi, Bhagwatikumar Sharma, Chandrakant Bakshi, Gunvant Shah, Harindra Dave, Harkisan Mehta, Jay Vasavada, Jyotindra Dave, Kanti Bhatt, Kavi Nanalal, Khabardar, Sundaram, Makarand Dave, Ramesh Parekh, Suresh Dalal, Tarak Mehta, Vinod Bhatt, Dhruv Bhatt and Varsha Adalja have influenced Gujarati thinkers.

A notable contribution to Gujarati language literature came from the Swaminarayan paramhanso, like Bramhanand, Premanand, with prose like Vachanamrut and poetry in the form of bhajans.

Shrimad Rajchandra Vachnamrut and Shri Atma Siddhi Shastra, written in 19th century by philosopher Shrimad Rajchandra (Mahatma Gandhi's guru) are very well known.

Gujarati theatre owes a lot to Bhavai. Bhavai is a folk musical performance of stage plays. Ketan Mehta and Sanjay Leela Bhansali explored artistic use of bhavai in films such as *Bhavni Bhavai, Oh Darling! Yeh Hai India* and *Hum Dil De Chuke Sanam*. Dayro (gathering) involves singing and conversation reflecting on human nature.

Famous Mumbai theatre veteran, Alyque Padamsee, best known in the English-speaking world for playing Muhammad Ali Jinnah in Sir Richard Attenborough's *Gandhi*, was from a traditional Gujarati-Kutchi family from Kathiawar.

CUISINE

Gujarati food is primarily vegetarian. The typical Gujarati *thali* consists of *rotli* or *bhakhari or thepala or rotlo*, *dal* or *kadhi, khichdi*, Bhat and *shak*. Athanu(Indian pickle) and *chhundo* are used as condiments.

Gujarati Thali

The four major regions of Gujarat all bring their own styles to Gujarati food. Many Gujarati dishes are distinctively sweet, salty, and spicy at the same time. In Saurashtra region, *chhash* (buttermilk) is believed to be a must-have in their daily food.

Cinema

The Gujarati film industry dates back to 1932, when the first Gujarati film, *Narsinh Mehta*, was released. After flourishing through the 1960s to 1980s, the industry saw a decline. The industry is revived in recent times. The film industry has produced more than one thousand films since its inception. The Government of Gujarat announced a 100% entertainment tax exemption for Gujarati films in 2005 and a policy of incentives in 2016.

Music

Gujarati folk music, known as *Sugam Sangeet*, is a hereditary profession of the Barot, Gadhvi and Charan communities. The omnipresent instruments in Gujarati folk music include wind instruments, such as *turi*, *bungal*, and *pava*, string instruments, such as the *ravan hattho*, *ektaro*, and *jantar* and percussion instruments, such as the *manjira* and *zanz* pot drum.

FESTIVALS

Garba during Navaratri in Ahmedabad

International Kite Festival, Ahmedabad

The folk traditions of Gujarat include bhavai and *raas-garba*. *Bhavai* is a folk theatre; it is partly entertainment and partly ritual, and is dedicated to Amba. The *raas-garba* is a folk dance done as a celebration of Navratri by Gujarati people. The folk costume of this dance is *chaniya choli* for women and *kedia* for men. Different styles and steps of *garba* include *dodhiyu*, simple five, simple seven, *popatiyu, trikoniya* (hand movement which forms an imagery triangle), *lehree, tran taali*, butterfly, *hudo*, two claps and many more Sheri garba is one of the oldest form of garba where all the ladies wear red patola sari and sing along while dancing. It is a very graceful form of garba. *Makar Sankranti* is a festival where people of Gujarat fly kites. In Gujarat, from December through to *Makar Sankranti*, people start enjoying kite flying. *Undhiyu*, a special dish made of various vegetables, is a must-have of Gujarati people on *Makar Sankranti*. Surat is especially well known for the strong string which is made by applying glass powder on the row thread to provide it a cutting edge. Apart from Navratri and Uttarayana, Diwali, Holi, Tazia and others are also celebrated.

Diffusion of culture

Due to close proximity to the Arabian Sea, Gujarat has developed a mercantile ethos which maintained a cultural tradition of seafaring, long-distance trade, and overseas contacts with the outside world since ancient times, and the diffusion of culture through Gujarati diaspora was a logical outcome of such a tradition. During the pre-modern period, various European sources have observed that these merchants formed diaspora communities outside of Gujarat, and in many parts of the world, such as the Persian Gulf, Middle East, Horn of Africa, Hong Kong and Indonesia long before the internal rise of the Maratha Dynasty, and the British Raj colonial occupation.

Early 1st-century Western historians such as Strabo and Dio Cassius are testament to Gujarati people's role in the spread of Buddhism in the Mediterranean, when it was recorded that the *sramana* monk Zarmanochegas of Barygaza met Nicholas of Damascus in Antioch while Augustus was ruling the Roman Empire, and shortly thereafter proceeded to Athens where he burnt himself to death in an act to demonstrate his faith. A tomb was made to the *sramana*, still visible in the time of Plutarch. The progenitor of the Sinhala language is believed to be Prince Vijaya, son of King Simhabahu who ruled Simhapura (modern-day Sihor near Bhavnagar). Prince Vijaya was banished by his father for his lawlessness and set forth with a band of adventurers. This tradition was followed by other Gujaratis. For example, in the Ajanta Frescoes, a Gujarati prince is shown entering Sri Lanka.

Many Indians had migrated to Indonesia, most of them being Gujaratis. King Aji Saka, who is said to have come to Java in Indonesia in year 1 of the Saka calendar, is believed by some to be a king of Gujarat. The first Indian settlements in Java Island of Indonesia are believed to have been established with the coming of Prince Dhruvavijaya of Gujarat, with 5000 traders. Some stories propose a Brahmin named Tritresta was the first to bring Gujarati migrants with him to Java, so some scholars equate him with Aji Saka. A Gujarati ship has been depicted in a sculpture at Borabudur, Java.

FLORA AND FAUNA

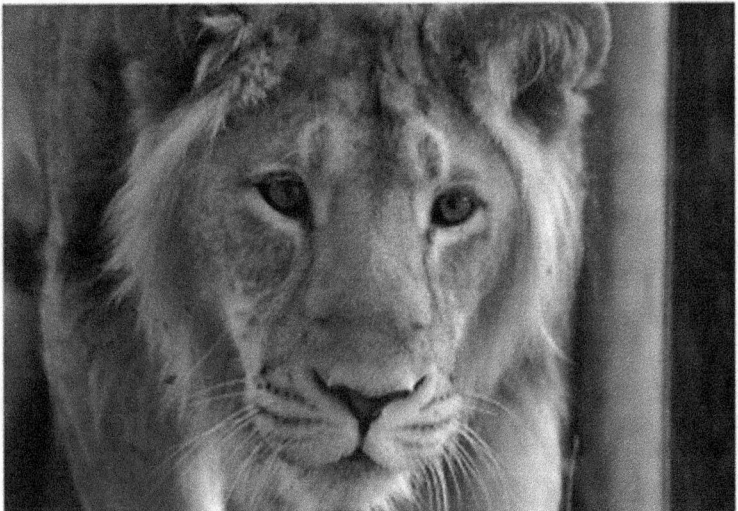

A young male Asiatic lion, which occurs in and around Gir National Park

Lesser flamingo, Jamnagar

Striped hyena at the Gir Forest National Park

According to the *India State of Forest Report 2011*, Gujarat has 9.7% of its total geographical area under forest cover. As per the districts, The Dangs has the largest area under forest cover.

Gujarat has four national parks and 21 sanctuaries. It is the only home of Asiatic lions and outside Africa, is the only present natural habitat of lions. Gir Forest National Park in the southwest part of the state covers part of the lions' habitat. Apart from lions, Indian leopards are also found in state. They are spread across the large plains of Saurashtra and the mountains of South Gujarat. Other National parks include Vansda National Park, Blackbuck National Park, Velavadar and Narara Marine National Park, Gulf of Kutchh, Jamnagar. Wildlife sanctuaries include: Wild Ass Wildlife Sanctuary, Nal Sarovar Bird Sanctuary, Porbandar Bird Sanctuary, Kutch Desert Wildlife Sanctuary, Kutch Bustard Sanctuary, Narayan Sarovar Sanctuary, Jessore Sloth Bear Sanctuary, Anjal, Balaram-Ambaji, Barda, Jambughoda, Khavda, Paniya, Purna, Rampura, Ratan Mahal, and Surpaneshwar.

Gujarat has some of the major mountain ranges of India, including Aravalli, Sahyadri (Western Ghats), Vindhya and Saputara. Apart from this Gir hills, Barda, Jessore, Chotila, etc. are situated in different parts of Gujarat. Girnar is the tallest peak and Saputara is the only hill-station in the state.

Indroda Dinosaur and Fossil Park, Gandhinagar

In the early 1980s, palaeontologists found dinosaur bones and fossils of at least 13 species Balasinor in Kheda District.

NOTABLE INDIVIDUALS

- Mahatma Gandhi, who spearheaded the Indian independence movement against British colonial rule, was a Gujarati.

- Sardar Vallabhbhai Patel Independent India's first Deputy Prime Minister and Home Minister, was from Karamsad.

- Morarji Desai, The 4th Prime Minister of India (1977–1979) who was from Valsad

- Vikram Sarabhai, who was "Father of the Indian Space Programme" came from a family of Jain industrialists from Ahmedabad.

- Shrimad Rajchandra, a revered Jain poet, philosopher and reformer best known as the spiritual guru of Mahatma Gandhi.

- Dhirubhai Ambani, founder of Reliance industries was from Chorvad, Gujarat.

- Azim Premji, software magnate and chairman of Wipro Limited is ethnically Gujarati.

- Pioneer industrialist Jamsetji Tata, who founded the Tata Group, one of India's biggest multinational conglomerates, came from a Parsi family of Zoroastrians in Navsari, and is considered the "Father of Indian Industry".

- Muhammad Ali Jinnah, revered in Pakistan as *Quaid-i-Azam* (Great Leader), *Baba-i-Qaum* (Father of the Nation) and first Governor general of Pakistan was from a Gujarati Muslim family in Rajkot.

- Narendra Modi, current Prime Minister of India is from Vadnagar, Gujarat.

- Urjit Patel, current Governor of Reserve Bank of India is from Kheda district, Gujarat.

2

Culture and Society

CULTURE OF GUJARAT

The Culture of Gujarat is both ancient and modern.

Gujarati engagement ceremony

In many Gujarati communities, the engagement ceremony is known as *Gaud Dhana*, which literally means "Jaggery and Corianderseeds" and refers to the practice of distributing a small amount of jaggery mixed with coriander seeds.

Gujarati Hindu wedding ceremony

Marriage is a highly auspicious occasion in Indian culture. According to the Vedas, the Hindu scriptures, marriage is a sacred lifelong commitment between a man and a woman. It is considered to be the strongest of all social bonds and is the initiation into a lifetime of togetherness.

The Vedic wedding ceremony consists of prayers, invocations, and vows recited in Sanskrit, the most ancient surviving language. The Vedic wedding ceremony dates back to over five thousand years and is performed under a decorated canopy, the *mandap*. The four pillars that surround the *mandap* represent the parents of the bride and groom. This signifies the important part they have played in raising their children to become the responsible adults they are today. The ceremony is performed before a sacred fire, or *agniaa*, which is the eternal witness of the marriage and all vows taken.

Parts of the ceremony

Every Hindu ceremony begins with the worship of Lord Ganesha, deity of peace and wisdom. This is done so people can find strength within themselves to remove any obstacles that may arise.

Varghodo (Wedding Procession)

The original form of a *barat* is a procession from the groom's house to the bride's house for the wedding ceremony. The wedding day begins with the Mangal Vadya, the playing of Shehnai (a traditional wind instrument) and Dhol (Indian drum).

Swagatam (Welcoming the groom and his family)

The groom and his family are greeted at the doors of the mandir (temple) by the bride's parents and family. The mother of the bride then greets and welcomes the groom and his family into her own family. She blesses the groom by placing a tilak (red dot) on his forehead. The groom is then led to the *mandap* where the wedding ceremony will take place.

Ganesh Puja (The worship of Lord Ganesh)

Madhuparka (Welcoming the groom)

While the groom is sitting under the *mandap* the *madhuparka* is performed where his feet are washed by the bride's parents. He is then offered *panchamrut*, a drink composed of milk, yogurt, ghee, honey, and sugar.

Kanyaa Daan (Giving away of the daughter)

The bride accepts her change of status from an unmarried woman to a wife by spreading turmeric powder on her hands. Kanya Daan is performed by the father (or uncle of guardian) of the bride in presence of a large gathering that is invited to witness the wedding.

Vivaaha (Wedding)

The bride and the groom face each other, and the priest ties their garments (the bride's saree to the groom's shirt) in a knot, symbolizing the sacred union. The bride and the groom garland each other and exchange the rings. Next the nuptial fire, symbolizing the divine witness, and the sanctifier of the sacrament, is installed and worshipped.

Both the bride and the groom grasp their hands together and pray to God for His blessings. Samagree, consisting of crushed sandalwood, herbs, sugar, rice, ghee (clarified butter), and twigs is offered into the sacred fire to seek God's blessings for the couple.

Mangal Phera (Circumambulation of the sacred fire)

The groom holds the bride by the hand and both walk three times around the sacred fire. Both offer oblations and recite appropriate Vedic hymns to Gods for prosperity, good fortune, and conjugal fidelity. They touch each other's heart and pray for union of their hearts and minds.

Saptapadi (Seven sacred steps)

This is the most important rite of the entire ceremony. Here the bride and the groom take seven steps together around the sacred fire (Agni) and make the following seven promises to each other: As per the Vedic rituals, the groom sings "With God as our guide, let us take":

1. The first step to nourish each other
2. The second step to grow together in strength
3. The third step to preserve our wealth
4. The fourth step to share our joys and sorrows
5. The fifth step to care for our children
6. The sixth step to be together forever
7. The seventh step to remain lifelong friends
8. The perfect halves to make a perfect whole!

The Satapadi ceremony concludes with a prayer that the union is indissoluble. At the end of this ceremony, the groom and the bride become husband and wife.

Mangal Sutra

The Mangal Sutra Dharana is the tying of the thread containing the marks of the Vishnu or Shiva on the neck of the bride by the groom.

Suhaag or Sindhoordana

The groom places sindoor (red powder) on the bride's hair symbolizing her as a married woman.

Aashirvaad (Blessing)

The groom's parents bless the couple and offer clothes or flower to the bride, symbolizing her joining the groom's family. All those assembled at the ceremony shower flowers on the couple and bless them completing the marriage.

Music and dance

Dandiya Raas is a romantic, very energetic, colourful and playful dance originating in the state of Gujarat. Its roots lay from the days of Lord Krishna who played raas on the shores of Yamuna river on a moonlit night with his beloved Gopis.

Men and women dressed in colorful clothes dance in two concentric circles - one moving clockwise, one moving counter-clockwise. Men and women carry two bamboo sticks called dandiyas in their hands. In addition to footwork, one of the most enjoyable part of this dance is the creative use of dandiyas.

The song sung on the occasion is essentially an amorous one. Raas is a very playful dance providing opportunity for acting and exchanging messages through eye contact. It is no wonder that many romances bloom during Navratri and hence the popularity of the dance among the younger generation.

Garba

Garba is a very graceful form of dance mainly performed by females in a circular formation, it is in reverences of goddess Ambaji. The basics of the dance are singing and clapping rhythmically while going around the goddess. Today many modifications are prevalent to the basic pattern and even men are free to join in. Women are dressed in exquisitely embroidered, set in mirrors cholis, ghaghras and bandhani dupattas! Extensive jewelry in the form of necklaces, bracelets and anklets are also worn. The typical dress code of men is kehediyu, chudidar and a turban.

Garbi

Originally men used to perform this dance. It was on the way back from a battle that the victorious army would start dancing to couplets and amorous songs sung by the Charanswar, or the narrators who used to go to the front to raise the spirit during the battle by singing songs of valour. The dance was characteristic for its forceful movements which would fascinate viewers. Today, however, even females participate in the dance.

Padhar

It is performed by a rural community living around Nal Lake. In it, performers simulate the rhythmic movements of roving mariners and the undulating sea waves. The Bhil tribes, who live close to border tracts, and the Adivasis of Dangs district, have particularly lively folk dances.

Theatre

The traditional forms of theatre include Bhavai and Akhyana.

Gujarati cinema

Before the arrival of talkies, there were several silent films which were closely related with Gujarati people and culture. Many film directors, producers and actors who are associated with silent films were Gujarati and Parsi. There were twenty leading film company and studios owned by Gujaratis between 1913 and 1931. They were mostly located in Bombay (now Mumbai). There were at least forty-four leading Gujarati directors during this period. The Gujarati cinema dates back to

9 April 1932, when the first Gujarati film *Narsinh Mehta* was released. *Leeludi Dharti* (1968) was the first colour film of Gujarati cinema. After flourishing through the 1960s to 1980s, the industry saw a decline. The industry is revived in recent times. The film industry has produced more than one thousand films since its inception. In 2005, the Government of Gujarat announced 100% entertainment tax exemption for Gujarati films.

Gujarati cinema is chiefly based on scripts from mythology to history and social to political. Since its origin Gujarati cinema has experimented with stories and issues from the Indian society. The films are generally targeted at rural audience but after recent revival also caters audience with urban subjects.

Languages of Gujarat

Gujarat is inhabited by people belonging to varied castes, religions and communities. Due to that, a number of varied languages are spoken in the state. The official language of the state is Gujarati. It is an Indo-Aryan language derived from Sanskrit. Gujarati is the 26th-most widely spoken language in the world. In addition, it has eleven dialects, spoken in different parts of the state.

Gujarat shares its borders with the states of Maharashtra, Madhya Pradesh and Rajasthan. Therefore, there is a small population which speaks the respective languages of the different states also, namely Marwari, Hindi, and Marathi. Apart from this, Urdu and Sindhi are also spoken in Gujarat. Kutch is one of the important areas in the state. It has an independent identity and is growing popular among tourists. The mother tongue of the people of Kutch is Kachchi. It is an important language of the region.

Another part of Gujarat is Saurashtra, which is also referred as West Gujarat or Kathiyawad. The mother tongue of this people is Kathiyawadi Gujarati which is spoken in seven different districts in Saurashtra. Rajkot is the financial capital of Saurashtra. Saurashtra is also known for giving many saints and great men like Mahatma Gandhi. Young population migrated to different cities like Ahmedabad, Surat and Vadodara due to employment problems.

Literature

Gujarati literature's history may be traced to 1000 AD. Since then literature has flourished till date. Well known laureates of Gujarati literature are Hemchandracharya, Narsinh Mehta, Mirabai, Akho, Premanand Bhatt, Shamal Bhatt, Dayaram, Dalpatram, Narmad, Govardhanram Tripathi, Mahatma Gandhi, K. M. Munshi, Umashankar Joshi, Suresh Joshi, Pannalal Patel and Rajendra Keshavlal Shah .

Kavi Kant and Kalapi are famous Gujarati poets. Gujarat Vidhya Sabha, Gujarat Sahitya Sabha, and Gujarati Sahitya Parishad are Ahmedabad based literary institutions promoting the spread of Gujarati literature. Saraswatichandra is a landmark novel by Govardhanram Tripathi. Writers like Suresh Dalal, Jyotindra Dave, Tarak Mehta, Harkisan Mehta, Chandrakant Bakshi, Vinod Bhatt, Kanti Bhatt, Makarand Dave, and Varsha Adalja have influenced Gujarati thinkers.

A huge contribution to Gujarati language literature came from the Swaminarayan paramhanso, like Bramhanand, Premanand, with prose like Vachanamrut and poetry in the form of bhajans.

Gujarati theatre owes a lot to bhavai. Bhavai is a musical performance of stage plays. Ketan Mehta and Sanjay Leela Bhansali explored artistic use of bhavai in films such as *Bhavni Bhavai, Oh Darling! Yeh Hai India!* and *Hum Dil De Chuke Sanam.* Dayro (gathering) involves singing and conversation reflecting on human nature.

Religions

In Gujarat, there have been several great religious figures. Sant Dadu Dayal (1554–1603), a saint-poet and a major Bhakti figure from Ahmedabad treated equally both Rama as names of God and became popular in Northern India. He wrote, "The illusion of Rama hath been dispelled by my mind; since I see Thee in all."

Gujarat is also the home of Gandhi who preached the unity between all religions and became a worldwide figure for peaceful struggle against tyranny.

Hinduism

Lord Ram, Laxman, and Sita Devi

Gujarat is a part of the ancient Indus Valley Civilization.

Many Hindu religious traditions developed in Gujarat. Gujarat is the birthplace of Lord Shiva's Avatar Lakulisa (*Staff-God*). He established the Pasupata Shaivite tradition (one of the six major schools of Shaivism) in 2 A.D. or 3 A.D. According to some traditions he was born in Kayarohana or Kayavatara in Saurashtra while other traditions hold that it was Karavana, in the modern-day town of Dabhoi Taluka near Baroda, another that it was Ulkapuri (modern Avakhal) and another that it was in Braoch or Bharuch. From Gujarat it spread north to Kashmir, South to Tamil Nadu, East to Nepal (where the Pashupatinath Temple stills exists popularly.)

Bhakti movement

The Bhakti movement was very popular in Gujarat where devotees of both Islam and Hinduism focused worship of God, trying to rid any separations based on faith in God.

Swami Chakradhara was another major figure of the Bhakti movement, born in Gujarat in 1194 A.D. and he is believed to be the avatar of Vishnu. Chakradhara Maharaja established the Manhubhava Vaishnavite sect which spread to Maharashtra as well. The sect still exists today in Gujarat and Maharashtra.

Sant Kilha was another Vaishnavite saint of Gujarat born to a Subedar (army man) father. He was the disciple of Krishnasdas (of Jaipur) and became his successor at the seat of Galta - Kilha's branch became known as the "Tapasa branch". Besides Ram Bhakti (devotion to Lord Rama), he was also inclined towards yog-saghana and this is why he was made acharya of the Galta Gaddi. He is said to be the founder of the Khati sect. Jalarama, a devotee of Lord Rama is another popular figure. Jalarama's birthday is still celebrated by Gujarati (in Gujarat and abroad) as Jalaram Jayanti.

Swami Sahajanand, better known as Swaminarayan settled in Gujarat from Uttar Pradesh. Today the Swaminarayan movement is very large in Gujarat.

Jainism

Gujarat is home to one of the largest Jain communities in India.

Shrimad Rajchandra was a Jain poet, philosopher, scholar and reformer, best known for his teachings on Jainism and as a spiritual guide of Mahatma Gandhi.

Gandhi's mother was also Jain.

Zoroastrianism

Zoroastrianism, first arrived in Gujarat, at around 9th century AD. Parsis migrated from Greater Iran to Gujarat and Sindh between the 8th and 10th century CE to avoid the persecution of Zoroastrians following the Muslim conquest of Persia.Since then, the Zoroastrians have flourished in the present day Gujarat and Mumbai. The holy cities of parsis are also located in Gujarat, like Udvad, their primary site.

Arrival in Gujarat : According to the Qissa-i Sanjan, the only existing account of the early years of Zoroastrian refugees in India composed at least six centuries after their tentative date of arrival, the first group of immigrants originated from Greater Khorasan. This historical region of Central Asia is in part in northeastern Iran, where it constitutes modern Khorasan Province, part of western/northern Afghanistan, and in part in three Central-Asian republics namely Tajikistan, Turkmenistan and Uzbekistan. According to the Qissa, the immigrants were granted permission to stay by the local ruler, Jadi Rana, on the condition that they adopt the local language (Gujarati), that their women adopt local dress (the sari), and that they henceforth cease to bear arms. The refugees accepted the conditions and founded the settlement of Sanjan, which is said to have been named after the city of their origin (Sanjan, near Merv, modern Turkmenistan). This first group was followed by a second group from Greater Khorasan within five years of the first, and this time having religious implements with them (the alat). In addition to these Khorasanis or Kohistanis "mountain folk", as the two initial groups are said to have been initially called, at least one other group is said to have come overland from Sari, Iran. This religion founded by Zarathustra Spitma (better known as "Zoroaster") resembles Hinduism in many ways (although differing as a strict monotheism too.)

For example, in this religion, the cow is very sacred. In the 9th chapter of the *Vendidad* of the *Avesta*, the purificatory power of cow urine is dilated upon. It is declared to be a panacea for all bodily and moral evils. It is drunk as well as applied externally as is done by Hindus also. Urine of the bull, called "nirang" is brought to the house of an orthodox Parsi every morning and is (like cow milk) applied to the face, hands and feet.

They Zoroastrians—a.k.a. Parsi and Irani, due to their ancient heritage—entered Gujarat from the Persian Empire.

They have many businesses in India and are economically very powerful.

Gujarati Muslims

The term "Gujarati Muslim" is usually used to signify an Indian Muslim from the State of Gujarat who speaks the Gujarati language as a mother-tongue (first language) and follows certain customs different from the rest of Indian Muslims.

Gujarat was one of the first places the Muslims came to India. King Arjun of Gujarat permitted a Muslim trader from Ormuz to build a mosque in Gujarat and even paid for the expenses of a certain Shiite festival. (p. 185 *An Advanced History of India* By Ramesh Chandra Majumdar, Kalikinkar Datta, Hemchandra Raychaudhuri)

The Sufi saints are very popular in Gujarat. Shaykh Makhu was a Sufi saint of the Shattari lineage (p. 185 *An Advanced History of India* By Ramesh Chandra Majumdar, Kalikinkar Datta, Hemchandra Raychaudhuri). Since Gujarat is situated on the western border of India, there was a direct interaction with people of Arabia and Persia. Many Gujarati Saints and Sufis became famous. Among them names of Sheikh Ganjul lim (1381), Syed Burhanuddin (1411) and Sheikh Wajihuddin Alviare well known.

Gujarati Muslims are very prominent in industry and sports, and there is a very large Gujarati Muslim community in Mumbai. Several Gujarati Muslim communities are:

- Memon
- Dawoodi Bohra
- Khoja
- Sunni Vora (aka "Vora Patel")
- Surti Muslims
- Pathan

There are many famous Gujarati Muslims:

- Muhammad Ali Jinnah
- Abdullah Yusuf Ali (translator and commentator of the Quran)
- Azim Premji (son of founder of multinational Wipro and current chairman)
- Badruddin Tyabji
- Ismail Merchant
- Tiger Memon (infamous)
- Irfan Pathan

- Yusuf Pathan
- Zaheer Khan
- Munaf Patel
- Sajid Nadiadwala
- Farooq Shaikh
- Parveen Babi
- Ismail Darbar

Fairs and festivals

Fairs

Around more than 1000 festivals are celebrated in Gujarat—the state is known as the land of fairs and festivals. Some of these fairs and festivals are as follows:

Bhavnath Mahadev Mela (February)

The Bhavnath Mahadev Temple, situated at the foot of Mount Girnar in the city of Junagadh, is the site of the Bhavnath Mahadev fair held for five days in February, during the festival of Mahashivratri. The Mahapuja of Lord Shiva takes place at midnight in this temple on the 14th day of the dark half of the month of Magh. When the puja (prayer ceremony)s , Naga Bavas (naked sages) living nearby move towards the fair seated on elephants, holding flags and blowing conch shells. It is firmly believed that Lord Shiva himself visits the shrine on this occasion. Visitors are served free meals by the organizers. Special stalls sell idols, rosaries, or holy beads (brought by vendors from Ayodhya and Mathura), utensils of brass and copper, sweets and fruits. The Bhavnath Mahadev Temple is surrounded by many equally ancient and holy places.

Dangs Darbar (March)

Dangs Darbar is the name of the annual fair held every year in Ahwa, the most important town in the Dangs a few days before Holi. The Dangs is one of the most delightful districts of Gujarat and is located high in the Saputara hills, the original

home of the adivasis, the tribal population of Gujarat. The name
"Darbar" dates back to the time of the British, when a darbar
of Rajas and Naiks of neighbouring area used to assemble there.
Today it is called Jamabandi Darbar, and the District Collector
officiates at it. Thousands of tribal people flock to Ahwa from all
over the district, dressed in bright colours, sounding the Shehnai,
and beating their drums. Folk dances, dramas, and songs enliven
the air during the festival.

Chitra — Vichitra Mela (March)

This fair, one of the largest purely Adivasi (tribal) fairs, is
attended by around 60,000 to 70,000 tribal people. It takes
place every year in the village of Gunbhakhari in Sabarkantha
district, very near the borders of Rajasthan. It is held a fortnight
after Holi, the festival of colours. The site of the fair is attractive
as the temple overlooks the rivers Sabarmati, Akul, and Vyakul.
The name of the fair is derived from Chitrangada and
Vichitraviraya, the sons of King Shantanu, who are believed
to have lived there and been cured of diseases which afflicted
them. The fair attracts large numbers of Bhils (tribals) who
come from all the surrounding districts using every imaginable
form of transport. The Garasis and Bhil tribals dress in their
customary colourful costumes. The costume of the men generally
consists of a blue shirt, dhoti, and a red or saffron turban.
Women don ghaghras (embroidered skirts), which have a
circumference of as much as 20 yards (18 m), and are covered
from head to foot with ornate and heavy silver jewellery. They
use liquid kumkum (vermilion) to colour their cheeks and lips
a brilliant red, while their eyes are outlined with kajal (kohl).
Every group that comes to the fair carries its own drum making
the atmosphere come alive with the incessant beat of numerous
drums. The women sing folk songs, and everyone dances. The
dancing and drumming continue for hours until everyone is
exhausted. Over a hundred stalls hold food and drink and
sweets of various kinds. Silver ornaments can be bought, and
household articles, as well. Here, as in other fairs, there is a
giant wheel and a merry-go-round which never ceases to spin.

Dhrang Fair (April)

Around 40 km from Bhuj, it is known for the samadhi of the famous saint Menkan Dada who served the community with great love and dedication and won their devotion. He was supposed to be the incarnation of Lakshmanji. A large fair is held on Magh Vad when a large number of Dada's followers from different parts of Gujarat and Rajasthan come to the Samadhi and participate in religious rituals.

Trinetreshwar Mahadev Fair (September–October)

The small hamlet of Tarnetar, about 75 kilometers from Rajkot, is the site for one of Gujarat's most well-known annual fairs, held here during the first week of Bhadrapad (September–October). This fair is primarily a "marriage mart" or "Swayamvar" for the tribal youth of today who still visit Tarnetar, to find them a suitable bride. The tribal youth elegantly dressed in colourful dhotis, waistcoats and eye-catching turbans come to be chosen by village belles dressed in colourful finery. Like all important tribal fairs, it is attended by tribes from the adjoining areas who indulge in dancing, competitive sports and other such forms of entertainment. There are over 300 stalls selling food, refreshments, exhibiting embroidery and cattle shows. The bachelors are usually identified by their large, colourful embroidered umbrellas and their distinctive hairstyles. These umbrellas, which have become emblems of the fair, are embroidered by the tribal youth for over a year. The fair is held around the Trinetreshwar Temple, which was dedicated to the three-eyed Lord Shiva and built at the beginning of the century. There is a kund (reservoir) here, and it is popularly believed that a dip in its waters is as holy as a dip in the sacred River Ganges. The reservoir is also known as papanshu (the destroyer of sins).

Vautha Mela (November)

This fair is held every year at Vautha where two rivers, the Sabarmati and the Vatrak, meet. Like most fair sites in India, this also has both mythological and current religious associations. The Vautha Mela site is 3 square miles (7.8 km) in area. Legends hold that Kartik Swami or Kartikeya, the son of Lord Shiva, visited the site. This is why the fair is held during Kartika Purnima, the full moon night of the month of Kartik, corresponding to November. The site, also known as Saptasangam, is at the confluence of seven rivers. The most important Shiva temple here is the temple of Siddhanath.

What is most significant about this fair is that it is the only major animal trading fair in Gujarat and is on par with the famous camel fair at Pushkar, Rajasthan. However, the only animals traded here are donkeys. About 4,000 donkeys are brought every year for sale, usually by Vanjara (gypsy) traders. The pilgrims who visit Vautha during the fair are from several communities and include farmers, labourers, and people belonging to several castes.

Shamlaji Melo (November)

The Shamlaji Melo, also called the Kartik Purnima fair is held in the month of November every year and lasts for about two weeks. It is attended by almost two hundred thousand people from adjoining districts and even from Rajasthan. Devotees belonging to various castes and communities including the Garasias and Bhils throng to this festival. These pilgrims come in groups, singing devotional songs and carrying religious banners to have a darshan (worship) of the deity at the Shamlaji Temple. The Shamlaji Temple is a renowned Vaishnav Shrine and the deity housed here is known by various names included Gadadhar (bearer of the mace) and Shaksi Gopal. The fair is also popular with the tribal people of the area, particularly the Bhils, who revere Shamlaji, the deity they refer to as "Kalio Bavji", the dark divinity. The temple is of great archaeological significance as it was built in the 11th century. Apart from a darshan of the deity in the temple, the pilgrims consider a bath in the river Meshwo essential.

Tarnetar Fair

The venkatareddy Tarnetar Fair is one of the most

happening events in Gujarat and is held at the Temple of Shiva or Trinetreshwar (three-eyed god), popularly known as Tarnetar. Popular belief associates the village with the Swayamwar (marriage) of Draupadi after Arjun performed the Mastsyavedh, an unparalleled feat of archery. Villagers from all over the state, dressed in their brilliant traditional costumes and exquisite jewellery, flock to Tarnetar. A veritable feast for the eyes is the Rasada, a captivating folk dance performed by hundreds of women moving gracefully in a single circle, dancing gaily to the accompaniment of four drums and jodja pava (double flutes). It is in district Surendranagar.

Kutch Utsav

The Kutch Mahotsava, is usually organised during the end of February and the beginning of March. The Kutch region in Gujarat abounds with splendid beaches, fascinating wildlife, and beautiful palaces and monuments.

Sanskruti kunj Fair

The Sanskruti kunj Festival shows the different cultures of the states of India. It is organised in the winter session in the capital city, Gandhinagar. All the competitors of India come during this fair and show their state's culture & dance.

It is 10 day long festival and this located on the bank of river Sabarmati over 12-hector landscaped land.Timing for sanskruti kunj between 2.00 pm to 10.00 pm and Every evening from 7.30 pm, the folk song and dance performances would be presented.

Shamlaji Fair

The Shamlaji shrine and the site boast of an ancient and glorious heritage. Thousands of tribal people flock to the Shamlaji fair. (Shamalaji also known as Gadadhar Dev whose Name is also reflected in Thousand Name of Lord Vishnu Also known as Vihnu Sahastra Nama Who Created Bhrahma And Bhrahma Created This World. Those Who had Crossed Bhrahma Is Known as Parbhrahma Who Claim Himself as Allah but He

Also Does not know that in Lord Vishnu Who seems to be idle in Whom Thousands Of Universe Takes Birth every moment and get destroy every moment and in its birth he is not happy neither he is unhappy in the destruction of all the universe. Still he fulfills the desire of Bhakta. Bhakta is he Who associates or joins himself with Lord vishnu who was also known as Shree Krishna. Famous Saint Narsimh Mehta Write Hundi On the Name Of Shmalia Sheth in the time of his distress a type of promissory note which was honored by Shree Krishna, Shri Narsimh Mehta wrote poetry in the honor of Shri Krishna which became Mahatma Gandhi's Prayer song.

Vautha No Melo

Situated at the confluence of two rivers near Ahmedabad, the site attracts people of all communities. Animals, particularly donkeys and camels, are sold in large numbers during this fair. parab vavdi fair (July) ashdhi 2

Festivals

Other than those festivals observed throughout India, there are festivities specific to Gujarat.

Makar Sankranti and Kite Flying Festival (14 January)

The Kite Flying Festival takes place in mid January and marks the time when the Sun's direct rays reach the Tropic of Capricorn after the winter solstice. It is celebrated with lots of folk music and dance as well as kite flying. People of Gujarat gather on terraces to fly kites of various colours to celebrate Makar Sakranti or Uttrayana, the welcome to the sun after the cold winter months. Glass strengthened threads of the Indian fighter kites are matched against each other in the air — the kite fighter who cuts the other thread is the victor. At night, kites with Chinese lanterns are flown and held aloft. Food such as Undhiya, sugar cane juice and local sweets is typically served to celebrate the day.

Dance Festival — Modhera (January)

Resting on a knoll in the village of Modhera are the ruins of the 11th century Sun Temple. The outer walls of the temple are covered with sculptures in which the figures of Surya, the sun god, are prominent. The Sun Temple is the site of an annual festival of Indian classical dances organized by the Tourism Corporation of Gujarat. The idea is to present classical dance forms in an atmosphere they were originally presented in.

The Kutch Mahotsav (February–March)

The 'Kutch Festival' or the 'Rann festival' is celebrated at the time of the Shiv Ratri in February/ March. The centre of the festival is Bhuj in Kutch. It has crafts, fairs and folk dances and music and cultural shows, all organized by the Gujarat Tourism. Tours are also conducted out to the ruins of Dhola Vera, a city that was once a part of the Indus Valley civilization.

Bhadra Purnima (September)

The full moon of Bhadrapad is one of the four most important festival days of the year when farmers and agriculturists come to Ambaji, a place that derives its name from Goddess Ambaji, whose shrine is located there. On this occasion, a large fair is organized on full moon days. In the evening, performances of Bhavai, the folk drama of the state, is held and Garba programmes are organized. The devout attend readings of the Saptashati, the seven hundred verses in praise of the goddess, and visit the temple for a darshan (worship) of her. The Ambaji shrine is the principal shrine of the goddess in Gujarat, and its origins are still unknown. The Temple of Ambaji is recognized as one of the original Shakti Pithas (religious texts) where, according to the ancient Scriptures, the heart of the goddess Ambaji fell to earth when her body was dismembered. A triangular Vishwa Yantra, inscribed with figures and the syllable 'Shree' in the centre, represents the deity. There is no idol, which testifies the temple's antiquity. Idol worship became popular much later.

Gujarati Cuisine

The food served in the South of Gujarat is influenced by the cuisine of Maharashtra. In South Gujarat, people usually consume Jowar, whereas in Saurashtra and North Gujarat, the diet consists mainly of Bajra and Maize. In Baroda, you will find a blend of all tastes due to its location. In earlier times, wheat was consumed only by the elite and by the middle class during the festive season. With changing time, things have changed. Today, wheat forms an integral part of the Gujarati platter and is used in a number of ways.

Sweets
- Basundi
- Doodh Pak
- Gajar ka Halwa
- Gulab Jambu
- Jalebi
- Ladoo
- Bundi na Ladoo
- Churm na Ladoo
- Tal na Lado
- Shing na Ladoo
- Dalia ni Chikki Shing Ni Chikki Tal ni Chikki(particularly for winter)
- Puran Puri
- Vedvi (similar to Puran Poli but fully dipped in ghee)
- ShriKhand (particularly in Summer)
- Mohan Thal
- Magas
- Barfi
- Ghari 1) Surati Ghari 2) Bhavnagari Ghari
- Sutarfeni
- Kaju Katri
- Golpapdi (jeggari and wheat-flour)

- Barfi Churmu
- Rabdi
- Khaja
- Dudhi no Halwo (and Mung Dal No Halwo Particularly for Marriage)
- Badam Ni Chaki(Particularly Offer to Lord Shrinathji of Nathdwara)
- Pista Ni Chaki(Particularly Offer to Lord Shrinathji of Nathdwara)
- Morning Sherow (Wheat Halwo)
- MaisurPack

Snacks

- Bhajias/Pakoras
- Pav Bhaji
- Chana Dal Wada
- Kutchi Dabeli
- Dal Wada
- Dhokla
- Farsi Puri
- Ganthias
- Handvo
- Kachori
- Khandvi
- Muthias
- Sev-Usual
- Bhel
- Panipuri
- Fafda
- Chevdo
- Bhakharvadi
- Chavanu
- Jain Chevdo
- Patra

- Gatha

Pulses (Dals)Kadhi

- Mixed Dal
- Moong Dal
- Plain Dal
- Tuver Dal
- Udad Dal
- Kadhi
- Dhal Dhokli

Vegetables

- Batata Suki Bhaji
- Cabbage Peas
- Cauliflower-Green Peas
- Methi Mutter
- Okra
- Sev-Tomatoes
- Undhiyu

The chewing of Betel leaves (paan) in Gujarat

The chewing of the betel leaf, known as *paan* in Gujarati, is part of many Asian cultures, especially those of China and Vietnam. Preparation techniques vary from using hands to feet to help in grinding and extracting the exotic flavours. The nut is either slivered or grated, often flavored with spices according to local tradition and usually wrapped in a betel leaf (betel leaf comes from the betel pepper plant, *Piper betle*, which is not botanically related to the betel palm, *Areca catechu*), along with some lime (calcium oxide or calcium hydroxide) to better extract the alkaloids. Some people also chew tobacco, marijuana or cocaine along with betel nut. After about 20 minutes of chewing, the fibrous residue which remains of the nut is spat out onto the street, where it remains visible due to its characteristic bright red color.

In Gujarat, betel (*paan*) chewing is as popular as tobacco

smoking is globally. Paan is often served wrapped in a betel leaf.

In Gujarat and the rest of India, paan has played an important part in social life and customs for hundreds of years. In the courts of Medieval Rulers, the betel leaf or paan was offered as part of hospitality, friendship and love. Kings also relished betel leaves after sex.

In Gujarat, an annual "Khemcho Majama" competition is held where the participants are rewarded based on their thook-cho art.

The different types of paans are:

- Saada paan, a mixture of cardamom, betel nut and cloves.
- Chutney paan, a mixture of cardamom, betel nut and spicy mint paste.
- Meetha paan, a mixture of grated coconut, dates, gulkand (rose petal and sugar syrup) and jellied fruit.
- thook paan, a special mixture of sugar and amylase
- Tobacco paan, a mixture of tobacco of different brands and betel nut.

Using paan with tobacco significantly increases the risk of mouth cancers. Even without tobacco, the use of paan has been associated with changes in the lining of the mouth that increase the risk of cancer of the mouth.

GUJARATI CUISINE

Gujarati cuisine refers to the cuisine of Gujarat, a state in western India. Despite having an extensive coastline providing wholesome seafood, Gujarat is primarily a vegetarian state due to the influence of Jain vegetarianism. Many communities, however, do include seafood, chicken, and goat in their diet.

The typical *Gujarati thali* consists of *rotli*, *dal* or *kadhi*, rice, and *shaak/sabzi* (a dish made up of several different combinations of vegetables and spices, which may be either spicy or sweet). The *thali* will also include preparations made from pulses or whole beans (called kathor in Gujarati) such as mung, black eyed beans etc., a snack item (*farsaan*) like dhokla, pathra, samosa etc. and a sweet (*mishthaan*) like mohanthal, jalebi, doodh pak etc. Gujarati cuisine varies widely in flavour and heat, depending on a family's tastes as well as the region of Gujarat to which they belong. North Gujarat, Kathiawad, Kachchh, Central Gujarat and South Gujarat are the five major regions of Gujarat that contribute their unique touch to Gujarati cuisine. Many Gujarati dishes are distinctively sweet, salty, and spicy simultaneously.

Staple foods

Staples include homemade *khichdi* (rice and lentil or rice and mung bean), and *chaas* (buttermilk) and pickles as side. Main dishes are based on steamed cooked vegetables with different spices and *dals* that are added to a *vaghar*, which is a mixture of spices heated in oil that varies depending on the main ingredients. Salt, sugar, lemon, lime, and tomatoes are used frequently to prevent dehydration in an area where temperatures reach 50 °C (122 °F) in the shade. It is common to add a little sugar or jaggery to some of the 'Vegetable dishes *and dal. The sweet flavour of these dishes is believed to neutralize the slightly bland taste of the vegetables.*

Gujarati Thali, a variety filled traditional dish served in Gujarat

The cuisine changes with the seasonal availability of vegetables. In summer, when mangoes are ripe and widely available in market, for example, *Keri no Ras* (fresh mango pulp) is often an integral part of the meal. The spices used also change depending on the season. *Garam masala* and its constituent spices are used less in summer. Regular fasting, with diets limited to milk, dried fruits, and nuts, is commonplace.

In modern times, some Gujaratis have become increasingly fond of very spicy and fried dishes. There are many chefs who have come up with fusions of Western and Gujarati food. Gujaratis are predominantly vegetarians, even though pockets of the state consume chicken, eggs and fish.

Flat bread prepared with Bajra has nutritional value similar to other foods based on flours. Common meals in villages near Saurashtra during the cold winters consists of thick rotis, termed *bhakri*, made of wheat flour, garlic chutney, onion, and *chaas*.

Sweets (desserts) served as part of a *thali* are typically made from milk, sugar, and nuts. "Dry" sweets such as magas and ghooghra are typically made around celebrations, such as weddings, or at Diwali.

Gujarati cuisine is also distinctive in its wide variety of *farsan* — side dishes that complement the main meal and are served alongside it. Some *farsan* are eaten as snacks or light meals by themselves.

Gujaratis will often refer to *dal-bhat-rotli-saak* as their everyday meal. For special occasions, this basic quartet is supplemented with additional *shaak*, sweet dishes, and *farsan*. A festive Gujarati *thali* often contain over a dozen items. Dietary rules restrict the permissible combination of dishes. For example, if *kadhi* is to be served, then a lentil preparation such as *chutti dal*, *vaal*, or *mug ni dal* will also be included. The sweet dish accompanying *kadhi* will likely be milk or yogurt–based, like *doodhpak* or *shrikhand*. However, a yogurt-based *raita* would not be served with such a meal. Festive meals based on *dal* will typically have a wheat-based sweet dish like *lapsi* or *ladoo* as the sweet accompaniment. Many Gujarati families make and consume *moong dal* in their diet on Wednesdays. There are established combinations of spices that some believe to facilitate digestion, that are eaten with different foods.

In coastal Gujarat, the *Kharwa* community has developed a cuisine consisting of fresh and dried fish. Common seafood are pomfrets, *khandwas*, *gedadas*, *surmai*, prawns, crabs, lobster. and *narsinga* (calamari).

Gujarati thali is sometimes seen as being "no-frills" even though it can be elaborate. India's current prime minister, Narendra Modi has often arranged Gujarati food for his special overseas guests like Shinzo Abe or Portuguese Prime Minister Antonio Costa Modi himself has been said to prefer Khichdi. even when visiting overseas, something that opposing politicians sometimes mocked.

Distinct Features

The Gujarati Cuisines vary in flavour and other aspects from region to region.You can notice that the food from Surat, Kutch, Kathiawad and North Gujarat are most distinct ones.Tastes also differ according to family preferences.Also most of the Gujarati popular dishes has the sweet taste.Traditionally sugar or jaggery is added to most of the Gujarati foods like vegetable and dal which gives it the sweet taste. Also the making style of Gujarati food is very unique. Some are stir-fried while some are steam cooked with vegetables and spices or dal being boiled and later vaghar (chaunk) being added to it to enhance it flavour.

List of Gujarati dishes

Breads

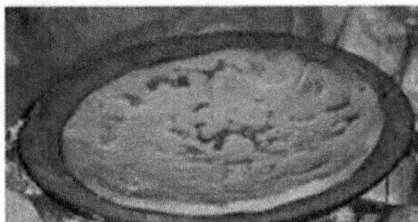

Bajri no rotlo

Puran Poli

- *Bajri no rotlo* (" "): Thick millet flour flatbread usually grilled over coals in clay pan.
- *Makai no rotlo*: Thick corn flour flatbread usually grilled over coals in clay pan.
- *Bhakri*: Made with whole wheat flour, thicker than *Rotli*, crispy.
- *Phulka rotli* (Also called *rotli* or *chapati*): Made with whole wheat flour, rolled thin.
- *Juvar no rotlo*: Thick sorghum flatbread.
- *Parotha*: Shallow fried whole wheat flatbread.
- *Puran poli* (Also known as *vedmi*): Whole wheat bread filled with sweet *Chickpea daal* filling usually made for special occasions.
- *Thepla/dhebra* ("/") : Made with a mixture of flours, pan fried, mildly spiced, usually contains shredded vegetables.
- *Poodla* (sweet): Made with a mixture of flours, pan fried.

Rice

In addition to plain rice, Gujarati cuisine also includes rice based dishes such as:

- *Biranj*: Steamed rice flavoured with saffron, sugar, and dried fruit.
- *Khatta-mittha bhaat* (sour and sweet rice): Rice, boiled with potatoes and spices, yellow in colour and accompanied with lemon peel.

- *Doodhpak*: Rice pudding made by boiling rice with milk and sugar, and flavoured with cardamom, raisins, saffron, cashews, pistachios, or almonds. It is typically served as a dessert.
- Khichdi (rice & a *dal*): Cooked like porridge accompanied with *ghee*, dahi (yogurt), and pickle.
- Pulao (rice with vegetables)
- *Khichu*: Kneaded rice flour made by heating it with water, salt, green chillies, and cumin.

*Vegetables (*Shaak*/)*

- *Bateta nu shaak* (potato curry)
- *Bateta sukhi bhaji* (dry potato)
- *Bateta Kanda nu shaak* (Potato and onion curry)
- *Bateta Ringan nu shaak* (Potato and Eggplant Curry)
- *Bateta Guvar nu shaak* (Potato and Cluster beans curry)
- *Bateta Chawli nu Shaak* (Potato and glossary long beans)
- *Lasaniya Bateta* (Garlic flavored Potato curry)
- *Bharela Ringan* (stuffed dry Eggplant)
- *Bharela bhinda* (stuffed dry okra)
- *Bharela karela* (stuffed dry karelu)
- *Bhinda nu shaak (dry okra)*
- *Bhinda Bateka nu shaak (dry Okra & potato)*
- *Vatana bataka nu shaak (potato and peas curry)*
- *Cholaa nu shaak* (black eyed peas curry)
- *Chawli Ringan Bateka nu Shaak* (glossary long beans, brinjal and potato curry)
- *Dhana capsicum nu shaak* (dry coriander, capsicum and chickpea flour curry)
- *Dudhi bateta nu shaak* (bottle gourd and potato curry)
- *Ringan bateta nu shaak* (eggplant and potato curry)
- *Dudhi chana ni daal nu shaak* (bottle gourd and split black chickpea curry)
- *Dudhi ganthia nu shaak* (bottle gourd)

- *Dudhi mag ni dal nu shaak* (bottle gourd and mung bean Curry)
- *Dudhi nu shaak* (bottle gourd curry)
- *Fansi ma dhokli nu shaak* (French bean curry with Dumplings)
- *Fansi nu shaak* (dry green bean curry)
- *Ganthia nu shaak*
- *Gathoda nu shaak*
- *Guvar nu shaak* (cluster beans curry)

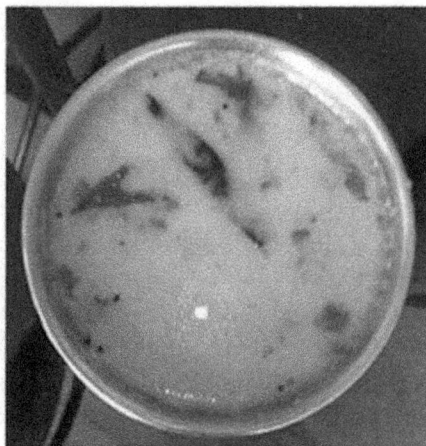

Kadhi

- *Kadhi* (curry made from buttermilk chhash and gram flour, usually either sweet or tangy)
- *Kanda bataka nu shaak* (onion and potato curry)
- *Karela nu shaak* (bitter melon curry)
- *Kobi bateta nu shaak* (dry cabbage and potato curry)
- *Keri nu shaak* (Mango curry)
- *Kobi Papdi nu shaak* (dry Cabbage and broad beans curry)
- *Mag nu shaak* (mung bean curry)
- *Methi nu shaak* (fenugreek)

- *Methi bateta nu shaak (fenugreeek potato curry)*
- *Panchkutiyu shaak* (five-vegetable curry consisting of ridge gourd, potato, bottle gourd, eggplant, and green peas)
- *Parwal bateta nu shaak* (pointed gourd and potato curry)
- *Ringan nu shaak* (eggplant)
- *Ringan no olo* (roasted eggplant mashed curry)
- *Sev tameta nu shaak* (curry made of green (unripe) tomatoes)
- *Sambhariyu Shaak* (Stuffed Ivy gourd, baby potatoes, sweet potatoes and eggplant curry)
- *Tameta bateta nu shaak* (tomato and potato curry)
- *Tindoda nu shaak* (ivy gourd curry)
- *Tindoda batetanu shaak* (ivy gourd curry)
- *Tameta muthiyanu shaak*
- *Palak nu shaak* (Spinach curry)
- *Undhiyu*: A mixed vegetable casserole that is traditionally cooked upside down underground in earthen pots fired from above. This dish is usually made of the vegetables that are available on the South Gujarat coastline during the winter season, including (amongst others) green beans, unripe banana, muthia, and purple yam. These are cooked in a spicy curry that sometimes includes coconut. *Surti Undhiyu* is a variant that is served with puri at weddings and banquets. Again it is a mixed vegetable casserole, made with red lentils and seasoned with spices, grated coconut, and palm sugar in a mild sauce. It is garnished with chopped peanutsand toasted grated coconut, and served with rice or roti. This dish is very popular all over Gujarat, and most Gujarati families eat it at least once a year on Makar Sankranti.
- *Val papadi nu shaak* (Flat bean)

Side dishes (Farsan)

Farsan are side dishes in Gujarati cuisine.
- *Dabeli* (A bread stuffed with the spicy masala mixture)

- *Bhajiya* (Deep fried savoury snacks. A popular variety is pakora.)

Khaman Dhokla

- *Dal Vada* (Deep fried savoury snacks. A popular variety is Dal Pakoda.)
- *Locho* (famous Surti variety made from chickpea flour)
- *Aloo Puri* (Another famous Surti variety)
- *Chaat* (A mixture of potato pieces, crispy fried bread, and spices topped with chutney, cilantro, and yogurt.)
- *Dahi vada* (Fried dumplings soaked in yogurt and topped with salt, cumin, and cayenne pepper.)
- *Dhokla* (Steamed cake made primarily of rice flour.)
- *Handvo* (Steamed cake made of rice flour, beans, yogurts, and calabash.)
- *Kachori* (A deep fried dumpling made of flour and filled with a stuffing of yellow moong dal, black pepper, cayenne pepper, and ginger.)
- *Khaman* (Steamed cakes made out of gram flour, garnished with green chili pepper and cilantro.) Types Of Khaman : Nylon Khaman & Vati Dal na Khaman

- *Khandvi* (Roll made of gram flour and dahi (yogurt) topped with mustard seed, cilantro, and Grated coconut.)
- *Upma*
- *Khichu* (A thick porridge-like mixture made of rice flour and seasoned with cumin seeds. Once prepared, the mixture is often topped with oil, cayenne pepper, and salt.)
- *Lilva kachori* (A variety of *kachori* made with pigeon peas.)
- *Patra* (Patarveliya)
- *Methi na gota* (Fried fenugreek Dumplings)
- *Muthia* (Steamed dumpling made of gram flour, fenugreek, salt, turmeric, and cayenne pepper. The steamed dumpling can also be stir fried with Mustard Seed.)
- *Pani puri* (A round hollow flatbread that is fried crisp and filled with potato, and black chickpeas and topped with water seasoned with mint and green chili pepper, and tamarind chutney.)
- *Sev khamani* (*Khaman* topped with crispy, fried gram flour.)
- *Vegetable handva* (Serve it hot either with chutney or tomato sauce or pickle.)
- *Dal vada, Vaati dal na bhajiya*
- *Makai no dana* (Corn chevda)
- *sabudana na vada*
- *Khichdo*
- Bhel

Snacks (Nasta)

Most *nasta* (singular *nasto*) are deep fried and made with Gram Flour.

- *Chakri*
- *Chorafali*
- *Fafda*

- *Ganthia*
- *Khakhra*
- *Mathia*
- *Sev (palak Sev, Aloo sev)*

Khandvi, a popular Gujarati snack (Farsan).

- *Sev mamra*
- *Lasaniya mamra*
- *Dhokla*
- *Porbandar khajli*
- *KHANDVI*
- *Methi sakarpara*
- *Methi Muthia*
- *Ragda Pettis*
- *Nachni Methi Muthias*
- *Tuver lilva kachori*
- *Khichu Papdi*

Dal *(pulses)*

- Moong Dal
- Meethi (Sweet) kadhi
- Kadh (an intermediate between kadhi and daal)
- Tuer dal
- Mix dal

Mithai *(sweets)*

Sukhadi

- *Adadiya*
- *Jadariyu*
- Sutarfeni
- Kansar
- Maisur
- Halvasan
- Malpua
- Keri no ras
- Basundi
- Ghari
- Ghughra
- Ghebar or Ghevar
- Son Papdi
- Magas (or Magaj)
- Sukhadi
- Mohanthar/Mohanthal (gram flour fudge)
- Gud papdi (Gol papdi)

- ghaum ni sev (wheat flour sev)
- Ronvelia
- Penda
- Barfi
- Ladu
- Shiro
- Ghooghra
- Jalebi
- Shrikhand
- Sweet Sev
- Lapsi
- Doodhpak
- Shakkarpara
- Kopra paak
- Gaajar halwo
- Dudhi no halwo gur
- Kaju katri
- Gulab jambu
- Velan lapsi
- Beet no halwo
- Moong dal Halwa Halwa

Condiments

- Chutney
- Raita
- Athanu
- Papadum or Papad
- Masala Papad
- Kachu
- Chhundo
- Murbbo
- Chhas (Buttermilk)

Spices and seasonings

- Kokum
- Aambli or Aamli (Tamarind)
- Goð (Jaggery)
- Chaat Masala
- Hardar or Havej (Turmeric powder)
- Kothmir (Coriander)
- Elaichi (Cardamom)
- Garam Masala (Mix of dry spices, roasted and made powder)
- Hing (Asafoetida)
- Jeeru (Cumin)
- Kesar (Saffron)
- Lilu marchu (Green chilli)
- Lal marchu (Cayenne pepper)
- Methi (Fenugreek - leaves and seeds)
- Phoodino or pudina (Mint)
- Soonth (ginger powder)
- Laving (cloves)
- Mitho limbdo (curry leaves)
- Dhanano (Coriander seeds)
- Singadana (Ground Nuts).

GUJARATI PEOPLE

The Gujarati people, or *Gujaratis*, is an umbrella term used to describe traditionally Gujarati speaking peoples who can trace their ancestry to the Gujarat region in India. Most of the Gujarati sub-ethnicities are of Indo-Aryan Ethno-linguistic extraction.

Origins: This region was the first to host upper caste Aryan-speaking peoples, and their descendants remain in the area. The Gujarati language has been adopted by communities such as the Kacchis, who use it as their literary language, and the Parsis, who had made the Gujarat region of the Indian subcontinent their home.

Present Status: People of the Gujarati ethnicity are primarily located in the northwestern part of the Indian subcontinent, specifically in the Gujarat, Rajasthan, Maharashtra, and Madhya Pradesh regions of India; in the former Portuguese-ruled parts of India—Daman and Diu and Dadra and Nagar Haveli, as well as in parts of Pakistan. The Gujaratis living in Pakistan are Muslims and are mainly those who migrated after the Partition of India and subsequent creation of independent Pakistan in 1947. They belong mainly to the Khoja, and Bohra groups. A large majority migrated to Karachi. A number of families still have relatives in Indian Gujarat and consider Gujarati to be their native tongue, even though they were born and brought up in Karachi. A point to be noted that memons who are often mistaken as Gujaratis are not actually Gujaratis and as their language and culture is different.

Due to a hard working and entrepreneurial spirit, many Gujaratis have done relatively well for themselves abroad.

FOOD

The majority of Hindu Gujaratis, and all Jain Gujaratis are vegetarian. Gujarati cuisine follows the traditional Indian full meal structure of rice, cooked vegetables (curry-like in texture) and bread. The bread is usually a *roti*. The different types of roti (breads) that a Gujarati cooks are roti, bhakhri, thepla, puri, maal purah and puran-pohli. Ghari and Khakhra are also eaten as roti, but they are usually eaten as a snack. Khaman, Dhokla, dhokli, dal-dhokli, undhiyu, fafda, chevdoh, papdi, bhusu and Sev mamra are Gujarati dishes savoured by many communities across the world. Use of Ghee in meals is very common. For example, pouring in rice or khichdi and applying on roti. The meal is usually accompanied with a sweet and a salty snack (*farsaan*) like Vada. Gujarati cookbook writers like Tarla Dalal are famous internationally.

The vegetable cooking involves preparing basic sauce first by frying masala with tomatoes and onions. Vegetables are usually added later. Gujaratis are more comfortable cooking with peanut oil (shing tel). However, while living abroad they adjust their cooking method with available Canola or Sunflower oil.

The making of masala is traditionally done on grinding stones. Nowadays, people use a blender or grinder to make masala. Each person makes masala differently, hence cooking tastes different depending on the household. People from north Gujarat use dry red chilli powder, whereas people from south Gujarat prefer using green chilli and corriander in their cooking. Gujarati Jains (and many Hindus) avoid using garlic and onions in their cooking. Traditionally Gujaratis eat Mukhwas or paan at the end of a meal. In many parts of Gujarat, having Chass butter milk or soda after lunch or dinner is quite common. Gujarati families celebrate Sharad Purnima by having dinner with doodh-pauva under moonlight.

Pakistani or Muslim Gujaratis are normally non-vegetarian.

DRESS AND JEWELLERY

Gujaratis change their dress according to the regional and local culture. Old wedding pictures of Gujaratis sometimes show the kurta (called zabbho) and pajama (called lehnghas). Kurtas have changed the appearance to more of national culture from regional culture. For quite some time, fashionable Gujarati ladies enjoyed wearing saris, but now they are switching to wearing the kameez at home and saris outside, wrapped in Gujarati style. Among men and women of the younger generations, western attire is becoming more common.

For jewellery and accessories, Gujarati ladies often hang a bunch of keys on the waist. The keyring holder is usually made in silver. Usual jewelry worn by ladies include the mangal sutra, necklace, earing, bangles, ring. With incidence of theft rising, cheaper costume jewelry is becoming more common. During weddings, Gujarati brides wear a lot of jewellery. It is common to see a Gujarati (Hindu) male wearing a gold chain and a ring. Married Gujarati (Hindu) women also traditionally wear a red 'bindi' (red powder worn in a round shape on the forehead also found in the form of stickers).

Every Hindu woman, married or not, wear 'bindi', married

woman wear red powder, called 'sindoor', on the forehead on or near the hairline. In addition to this they will also wear the 'bindi' or 'tika'. During the wedding the priest will have the groom put the first red powder on the bride. Some more traditional woman still apply this red power to their forehead each morning.

The red power, 'sindoor', is not in a round shape but is rubbed on the forehead near the hairline. The stickers are 'bindi' and any woman, married or not, wear these in many different colours and usually come in the form of a sticker and may match the girl's/woman's outfits in colour and design.

3

Government and Politics

POLITICS OF GUJARAT

On 1 May 1960, the Indian State of Gujarat was created out of the 17 northern districts of former State of Bombay. These districts were later further subdivided. There are 33 administrative districts in the state (as of 2018). Unlike other cities, Gandhinagar has its own administrative body, 'The Capital Project division', created by the Government of Gujarat in 1965 for Balanced & Deciplinate System in Gandhinagar capital city.

Gujarat is governed by a Legislative Assembly of 182 members. Members of the Legislative Assembly (MLA) are elected on the basis of adult suffrage from one of 182 constituencies, of which 13 are reserved for scheduled castes and 26 for scheduled tribes. The term of office for a member of the Legislative Assembly is five years. The Legislative Assembly elects a speaker, who presides over the meetings of the legislature. A governor is appointed by the President of India, and is Assembly, and to address the House after every general election and the commencement of each year's first session of the Legislative Assembly. The leader of the majority party or coalition in the legislature (Chief Minister) or his or her designee acts as the Leader of the Legislative Assembly. The administration of the state is led by the Chief Minister.

Vallabhbhai Patel, born in Nadiad in 1875, was independent

India's first Deputy Prime Minister and Home Minister; he played a key role in political integration of India, and was conferred with a posthumous Bharat Ratna award in 1991.

After gaining independence in 1947, the Indian National Congress party (INC) ruled the Bombay state (which included present-day Gujarat and Maharashtra). Congress continued to govern Gujarat after the state's creation in 1960. During and after India's State of Emergency of 1975-1977, public support for the Congress Party eroded, but it continued to hold government until 1990. In the 1990 Assembly Polls, the Congress lost to the janta dal-Bharatiya Janata Party (BJP) and chimanbhai patel came to power. 1995 BJP won assembly election & keshbhau patel was CM. His Government lasted only two years. The fall of that government was provoked by a split in the BJP led by Shankersinh Vaghela has won most of the subsequent polls. In 2001, following the loss of two assembly seats in by-elections, Keshubhai Patel resigned and yielded power to Narendra Modi. The BJP retained a majority in the 2002 election, and Narendra Modi has since served as Chief Minister of the state. On 1 June 2007, Narendra Modi became the longest serving Chief Minister of Gujarat. BJP retained a majority once again in polls (Dec, 2012) and Narendra Modi became Chief Minister.

In the Indian general election, 2014, Bharatiya Janta Party projected Narendra Modi as a candidate of Prime Minister. BJP retained clear majority first time in center and Narendra Modi become Prime Minister. So he resigned and yielded power to Anandiben Patel. She became the first lady Chief Minister of Gujarat. Vijay Rupanisucceeded her in August 2016.

Chief Ministers

Gujarat has had 16 different Chief Ministers since its formation in 1960. From 1960 until 1995 they were all from the Indian National Congress party, except for eight years when the opposition Janata Party/Janata Dal ruled. Since 1995, however, the Bharatiya Janata Party has dominated, controlling the Chief Minister for all except 18 months.

Revenues of government

This is a chart of trend of own tax revenues (excluding the shares from Union tax pool) of the Government of Gujarat assessed by the Finance Commissions from time to time with figures in millions of Indian Rupees.

Year	Own tax revenues
2000	104,818
2005	138,964

This is a chart of trend of own non-tax revenues (excluding the shares from Union tax pool) of the Government of Gujarat assessed by the Finance Commissions from time to time with figures in millions of Indian Rupees.

GOVERNANCE AND ADMINISTRATION

Gandhinagar, the capital of Gujarat State. The picture shown above is of the Legislative Assembly and seat of Gujarat government.

Gujarat is governed by a Legislative Assembly of 182 members. Members of the Legislative Assembly are elected on the basis of adult suffrage from one of 182 constituencies, of which 13 are reserved for scheduled castes and 27 for scheduled tribes. The term of office for a member of the Legislative Assembly is five years. The Legislative Assembly elects a speaker who presides over the meetings of the legislature. A governor is appointed by the President of India, and is to address the state legislature after every general election and the commencement of each year's first session of the Legislative Assembly. The leader of the majority party or coalition in the legislature (Chief Minister) or his or her designee acts as the Leader of the Legislative Assembly. The administration of the state is led by the Chief Minister.

After the independence of India in 1947, the Indian National Congress (INC) ruled the Bombay State (which included present-day Gujarat and Maharashtra). Congress continued to govern Gujarat after the state's creation in 1960.

During and after India's State of Emergency of 1975–1977, public support for the INC eroded, but it continued to hold government until 1995 with brief rule of nine months by Janata Morcha. In the 1995 Assembly elections, the Congress lost to the Bharatiya Janata Party (BJP) led by Keshubhai Patel who became the Chief Minister. His government lasted only two years. The fall of that government was provoked by a split in the BJP led by Shankersinh Vaghela. BJP again won election in 1998 with clear majority. In 2001, following the loss of two assembly seats in by-elections, Keshubhai Patel resigned and yielded power to Narendra Modi. BJP retained a majority in the 2002 election, and Narendra Modi remained as Chief Minister. On 1 June 2007, Narendra Modi became the longest serving Chief Minister of Gujarat. BJP retained the power in subsequent elections in 2007 and 2012 and Narendra Modi continued as the Chief Minister. After Narendra Modi became the Prime Minister of India in 2014, Anandiben Patel became the first female Chief Minister of the state.Vijay Rupani took over as Chief Minister and Nitin Patel as Dy. Chief Minister on 7 August 2016 after Anandiben Patel resigned earlier on 3 August.

GOVERNMENT OF GUJARAT

The Government of Gujarat, also known as the State Government of Gujarat, or locally as State Government, is the supreme governing authority of the Indian state of Gujarat and its 33 districts. It consists of an executive, led by the Governor of Gujarat, a judiciary and a legislative branch. Like other states in India, the head of state of Gujarat is the Governor, appointed by the President of India on the advice of the Central government. His or her post is largely ceremonial. The Chief Minister is the head of government and is vested with most of the executive powers. Gandhinagar is the capital of Gujarat, and houses the Vidhan Sabha(Legislative Assembly) and the secretariat. The Gujarat High Court, located in Ahmedabad, has jurisdiction over the whole state.

The present Legislative Assembly of Gujarat is unicameral, consisting of 182 Member of the Legislative Assembly(M.L.A). Its term is 5 years, unless sooner dissolved.

GUJARAT LEGISLATIVE ASSEMBLY

Gujarat Legislative Assembly or Gujarat Vidhan Sabha is the unicameral legislature of the Indian state of Gujarat. It is situated in the capital Gandhinagar. Presently, 182 members of the Legislative Assembly are directly elected from the single-seat constituencies and one member is nominated. It has term of 5 years unless it is dissolved sooner. 13 constituencies are reserved for scheduled castes and 27 constituencies for scheduled tribes.

History

Bhavsinhji Gohil, ruler of Bhavnagar State, established *The Peoples' Representative Assembly* consisting of 38 members appointed by him. His succeeding son, Krishnakumar Sinhji, formed the Bhavnagar legislative assembly in 1941 having 55 members, consisting of 33 elected members, 16 nominated members by him and 6 ex-officio members. They had power to ask questions, move resolutions, discuss the budget and introduce bills in the assembly. This assembly used to meet at least twice in a year. Porbandar state assembly had same powers. Sayajirao Gaekwad III, ruler of Baroda State, had formed the Baroda legislative assembly in 1908.

Since 1921, representative were elected by the people of that area of the present Gujarat state except the princely states, and sent to the Bombay State legislative assembly. In 1952, Saurashtra State legislative assembly was constituted after the independence of India. It was functional till 31 October 1956. Saurashtra State was merged into the Bombay State under the States Reorganization Act, 1956.

On 1 May 1960, the Bombay State was bifurcated into Gujarat and Maharashtra states which resulted in formation of Gujarat legislative assembly. The 132 members of the former Bombay legislative assembly, elected from the territorial constituencies of Gujarat, formed the first Gujarat legislative assembly. The number of the members was increased to 154 in 1962, 168 in 1967 and 182 in 1975.

Location

After formation of Gujarat state in 1960, Ahmedabad was a capital of the state. The Assembly started functioning from the present day OPD building of Ahmedabad Civil Hospital. The new capital city, Gandhinagar was built in 1971. Later assembly was shifted to Central Library building, sector-17, Gandhinagar on 11 February 1971. The new assembly building, Vithalbhai Patel Bhavan, was completed and inaugurated in 1982. Since then the Gujarat legislative assembly functions there.

Building

President Neelam Sanjiva Reddy laid foundation stone of new assembly building, Vithalbhai Patel Bhavan on 20 March 1978. It was designed by H. K. Mewada, chief planner of Gandhinagar. The construction was completed in July 1982 and it is named after Vithalbhai Patel, the first Indian speaker of Central Legislative Assembly during the British period. It was inaugurated by the Governor Sharda Mukherjee on 8 July 1982.

It is constructed with Reinforced concrete and the outer walls of the building is affixed with Dholpur light pink stones. The building is constructed on the 133 square metre platform amid a water pool having diameter of 200 metres. This central building was linked with the Ministerial Secretariat by bridges formerly but now new buildings are constructed in between known as Swarnim Sankul. The building is 33.45 metres high including its octagonal dome. The constructed area of building is 8100 square metres while the total built up area of square platform is 17689 square metres. It has four floors with total built up area of 43350 square metres or total carpet area of 16180 square

metres. The entrance of the building is reached by a flight of
steps. The Assembly hall is situated on the second floor. It is
octagonal from inside. The octagonal roof is supported by eight
V-shaped pillars and one pillar in the centre. These pillars tapers
and forms octagonal dome on the hall. There is an arrangement
of white floodlights on the top. The hall has a capacity of 232
seats though currently the assembly has only 182 elected members.
The hall is viewed from the galleries on the third floor which has
a capacity of 564 seats. There is a podium just under the Assembly
hall which is used for ceremonies and functions. The downward
floor of the Assembly hall makes an umbrella-like roof of the
podium. The podium has some personal belongings of Mahatma
Gandhi and Vallabhbhai Patel on display. There are oil paintings
of several national leaders, independence activists and personalities
on its walls. It was constructed at the cost of 6 crores. The
assembly building along with other government offices is situated
in Sector 10 of Gandhinagar. This capitol complex is spread in
area of 370 acres.

History of elections

List of Speakers

Name	Term
Kalyanji V. Mehta	1 May 1960 – 19 August 1960
Mansinhji Rana	19 August 1960 – 19 March 1962
Fatehali Palejwala	19 March 1962 – 17 March 1967
Raghavji Leuva	17 March 1967 – 28 June 1975
Kundanlal Dholakia	28 June 1975 – 28 March 1977
Manubhai Palkhiwala (Acting Speaker)	28 March 1977 – 21 April 1977
Kundanlal Dholakia	21 April 1977 – 20 June 1980
Natwarlal Shah	20 June 1980 – 8 January 1990
Karsandas Soneri (Acting Speaker)	8 January 1990 – 19 January 1990
Barjorji Pardiwala	19 January 1990 – 16 March 1990
Shashikant Lakhani	16 March 1990 – 12 November 1990
Manubhai Parmar	

(Acting Speaker)	12 November 1990 – 11 February 1991
Himatlal Mulani	11 February 1991 – 21 March 1995
Harishchandra Patel	21 March 1995 – 16 September 1996
Chandubhai Dabhi	
(Acting Speaker)	16 September 1996 – 29 October 1996
Gumansinhji Vaghela	29 October 1996 – 19 March 1998
Dhirubhai Shah	19 March 1998 – 27 December 2002
Prof. Mangaldas Patel	27 December 2002 – 18 January 2008
Ashok Bhatt	18 January 2008 – 29 September 2010
Prof. Mangaldas Patel	
(Acting Speaker)	29 September 2010 – 23 Feb 2011
Ganpat Vasava	23 February 2011 – 26 December 2012
Vajubhai Vala	
(Acting Speaker)	26 December 2012 - 19 January 2013
Neema Acharya	
(Acting Speaker)	19 January 2013 – 22 January 2013
Vajubhai Vala	23 January 2013 - 30 August 2014
Mangubhai C. Patel	
(Acting Speaker)	30 August 2014 – 9 November 2014
Ganpat Vasava	9 November 2014 – 7 August 2016
Parbatbhai Patel	
(Acting Speaker)	7 August 2016 – 22 August 2016
Ramanlal Vora	22 August 2016 - 16 February 2018
Rajendra Trivedi	16 February 2018 - Incumbent

COUNCIL OF MINISTERS OF GUJARAT

Council of Ministers of Gujarat (Gujarati: " ") exercises executive authority of the Indian State of Gujarat. The council is chaired by the Chief Minister of Gujarat. The council serves as the highest decision-making body in the State of Gujarat and advises the Governor of Gujarat in the exercise of his or her functions. The Council of Ministers is responsible to the Gujarat Legislative Assembly.

Constitutional Provisions

Article 163 of the Constitution of India makes provision for the State Governments of the Republic of India to have a

Council of Ministers, headed by a Chief Minister, so as to aid and assist that state's Governor in the exercise of his or her functions. While the Governor is the executive Head of the State, actual executive power can only be exercised after a consensus is reached by the Council of Ministers.

Upon being so advised, the Governor is expected to act accordingly.

The Governor of Gujarat appoints the Chief Minister of Gujarat. Ministers serving on the Council, in turn, are appointed by the Governor under advisement by the Chief Minister. While a Council Minister technically holds office at the pleasure of the State Governor, practically, a sitting Minister may be removed by the Governor only after consulting with, and receiving advice from, the Chief Minister.

Both the Chief Minister and those serving on the Council of Ministers must also be members of the Gujarat Legislative Assembly. If he or she is not a Member of the Legislative Assembly (MLA), he or she shall obtain membership of the assembly within six months of his or her appointment. The Council is collectively responsible to the Legislative Assembly and holds office till they enjoy the confidence of the Gujarat Legislative Assembly. Alternatively, a serving Council Minister may be removed by the Legislative Assembly through passage of a no confidence motion. As per Article 164 (1A) of the Constitution of India, the maximum strength of the Council of Ministers in Gujarat will be fifteen percent of the total Legislative Assembly strength . Hence, considering that the total strength of the Legislative Assembly of Gujarat is 182 members, the State's Council of Ministers may only be served by no more than forty-three members.

Types of Ministers

The Gujarat Council of Ministers follows the westminster's model of cabinet. There are two type of ministers.

- Cabinet Ministers.
- Ministers of State.

Cabinet Ministers

Actual power of decisions vests with cabinet ministers. The cabinet is chaired by the Chief Minister.

Ministers of State

They are also known as Deputy Ministers. They are appointed to assist cabinet ministers. However, many times, they are given independent charge of their department. In that case, they enjoy a latitude for decision making similar to a cabinet minister, with respect to those decisions under the aegis of their respective departments. However, Ministers of State do not participate in cabinet meetings.

Present Council of Ministers

Vijay Rupani second ministry.

INDIAN POLITICAL PARTIES

Gujarat Janata Congress

Gujarat Janata Congress (Gujarat Popular Congress), a political party in the Indian state of Gujarat. GJC was launched by former Congress Chief Minister, Chhabildas Mehta on May 9, 2001. Another important leader of GJC is Indubhai Patel.

Janata Dal (Gujarat)

Janata Dal (Gujarat) was a splinter-group of Janata Dal in Gujarat. This group was led by Chhabildas Mehta and Chimanbhai Patel. It was later dissolved and its leaders joined the Indian National Congress.

4

Language and Literature

GUJARATI LANGUAGE

Gujarati is an Indo-Aryan language native to the Indian state of Gujaratand spoken predominantly by the Gujarati people. Gujarati is part of the greater Indo-European language family. Gujarati is descended from Old Gujarati (*circa* 1100–1500 AD). In India, it is the official language in the state of Gujarat, as well as an official language in the union territories of Daman and Diu and Dadra and Nagar Haveli. As of 2011, Gujarati is the 6th most widely spoken language in India by number of native speakers, spoken by 55.5 million speakers which amounts to about 4.5% of the total Indian population. It is the 26th most widely spoken language in the world by number of native speakers as of 2007.

The Gujarati language is more than 700 years old and is spoken by more than 55 million people worldwide. Outside of Gujarat, Gujarati is spoken in many other parts of South Asia by Gujarati migrants, especially in Mumbai and Pakistan(mainly in Karachi). Gujarati is also widely spoken in many countries outside South Asia by the Gujarati diaspora. In North America, Gujarati is one of the fastest growing and most widely-spoken Indian languages in Canada and the United States. In Europe, Gujaratis form the second largest of the British South Asian speech communities, and Gujarati is the fourth most commonly spoken language in the U.K.'s capital London. Gujarati is also spoken in Southeast Africa, particularly in Kenya, Uganda, Tanzania, Zambia and South Africa. Elsewhere, Gujarati is spoken to a lesser extent in China (particularly Hong Kong), Indonesia, Singapore, Australia and Middle Eastern countries such as Bahrain. Gujarati was the mother tongue of Mahatma Gandhi and Muhammad Ali Jinnah.

History

Gujarati (also sometimes spelled *Gujerati, Gujarathi, Guzratee, Guujaratee*, "Gujarati", *Gujrathi*, and *Gujerathi*) is a modern IA (Indo-Aryan) language evolved from Sanskrit. The traditional practice is to differentiate the IA languages on the basis of three historical stages:

1. Old IA (Vedic and Classical Sanskrit)
2. Middle IA (various Prakrits and Apabhramshas)
3. New IA (modern languages such as Hindi, Punjabi, Bengali, etc.)

Another view postulates successive family tree splits, in which Gujarati is assumed to have separated from other IA languages in four stages:

1. IA languages split into Northern, Eastern, and Western divisions based on the innovate characteristics such as plosives becoming voiced in the Northern (Skt. *danta* "tooth" > Punj. *dând*) and dental and retroflex sibilantsmerging with the palatal in the Eastern (Skt. *sandhya* "evening" > Beng. *úâjh*).
2. Western, into Central and Southern.
3. Central, in Gujarati/Rajasthani, Western Hindi, and Punjabi/Lahanda/Sindhi, on the basis of innovation of auxiliary verbs and postpositions in Gujarati/Rajasthani.
4. Gujarati/Rajasthani into Gujarati and Rajasthani through development of such characteristics as auxiliary *ch-* and the possessive marker *-n-* during the 15th century.

The principal changes from Sanskrit are the following:

• Phonological

- Loss of original phonemic length for vowels
- Change of consonant clusters to geminate and then to single consonants (with compensatory vowel length)

English	Sanskrit	Prakrit	Gujarati
hand	*hasta*	*hattha*	*hâth*
seven	*sapta*	*satta*	*sât*
eight	*acm â*	*amm ha*	*âm h*
snake	*sarpa*	*sappa*	*sâp*

- Morphological
- Reduction in the number of compounds
- Merger of the dual with plural
- Replacement of case affixes by postpositions
- Development of periphrastic tense/voice/mood constructions
- Syntax
- Split ergativity
- More complex agreement system

Gujarati is then customarily divided into the following three historical stages:

Modern Gujarati (AD 1800 – present)

A major phonological change was the deletion of final ə, such that the modern language has consonant-final words. Grammatically, a new plural marker of -o developed. In literature, the third quarter of the 19th century saw a series of milestones for Gujarati, which previously had had verse as its dominant mode of literary composition.

Demographics and distribution

Of the approximately 46 million speakers of Gujarati in 1997, roughly 45.5 million resided in India, 150,000 in Uganda, 50,000 in Tanzania, 50,000 in Kenya and roughly 100,000 in Karachi, Pakistan, excluding several hundreds of thousands of

Memonis who do not self-identify as Gujarati, but hail from a region within the state of Gujarat. However, Gujarati community leaders in Pakistan claim that there are 3 million Gujarati speakers in Karachi. Elsewhere in Pakistan, Gujarati is also spoken in Lower Punjab. Pakistani Gujarati is probably a dialect of Gamadia.

There is a certain amount of Mauritian population and a large amount of Réunion Island people who are from Gujarati descent among which some of them still speak Gujarati.

A considerable Gujarati-speaking population exists in North America, most particularly in the New York City Metropolitan Areaand in the Greater Toronto Area, which have over 100,000 speakers and over 75,000 speakers, respectively, but also throughout the major metropolitan areas of the United States and Canada. According to the 2011 census, Gujarati is the seventeenth most spoken language in the Greater Toronto Area, and the fourth most spoken South Asian language after Hindi-Urdu, Punjabi and Tamil.

The UK has over 200,000 speakers, many of them situated in the London area, especially in North West London, but also in Birmingham, Manchester, and in Leicester, Coventry, Bradford and the former mill towns within Lancashire. A portion of these numbers consists of East African Gujaratis who, under increasing discrimination and policies of Africanisation in their newly independent resident countries (especially Uganda, where Idi Amin expelled 50,000 Asians), were left with uncertain futures and citizenships. Most, with British passports, settled in the UK.Gujarati is offered as a GCSE subject for students in the UK.

Gujarati parents in the diaspora are not comfortable with the possibility of their language not surviving them. In a study, 80% of Malayali parents felt that "Children would be better off with English", compared to 36% of Kannadaparents and only 19% of Gujarati parents.

Besides being spoken by the Gujarati people, non-Gujarati residents of and migrants to the state of Gujarat also count as speakers, among them the Kutchis (as a literary language), the Parsis (adopted as a mother tongue), and Hindu Sindhi refugees from Pakistan. A distribution of the geographical area can be found in 'Linguistic Survey of India' by George A. Grierson.

Official status

Gujarati is one of the twenty-two official languages and fourteen regional languages of India. It is officially recognized in the state of Gujarat, India and the union territories of Dadra and Nagar Haveli and Daman and Diu.

Gujarati is recognized and taught as a minority language in the states of Rajasthan, Madhya Pradesh, Maharashtra, and Tamil Nadu and the union territory of Delhi.

Dialects

According to British historian and philologist William Tisdall, who was an early scholar of Gujarati grammar, three major varieties of Gujarati exist: a standard 'Hindu' dialect, a 'Parsi' dialect and a 'Muslim' dialect.

However, Gujarati has undergone contemporary reclassification with respect to the widespread regional differences in vocabulary and phrasing; notwithstanding the number of poorly attested dialects and regional variations in naming.

- Standard Gujarati: this forms something of a standardised variant of Gujarati across news, education and government. It is also spoken in pockets of Maharashtra. The varieties of it include Mumbai Gujarati, Nagari, Patnuli, Saurashtra Standard.

- Gamadia: spoken primarily in Ahmedabad and the surrounding regions, in addition to Bharuch and Surat, where it is colloquially known as 'Surati'. The varieties of it include Ahmedabad Gamadia, Anawla, Brathela, Charotari, Eastern Broach Gujarati, Gramya, Patani, Patidari, Surati, Vadodari.

- Kathiawari: a distinctive variant spoken primarily in the Kathiawar region and subject to significant Sindhi influence. The varieties of it include Bhavnagari, Gohilwadi, Holadi/ Halari, Jhalawadi, Sorathi.

Kharwa, Kakari and Tarimuki (Ghisadi) are also often cited as additional varieties of Gujarati.

- Parsi: spoken by the Zoroastrian Parsi minority. This highly distinctive variety has been subject to considerable lexical influence by Avestan, the liturgicalZoroastrian language.

- Lisan ud-Dawat: spoken primarily by Gujarati Muslim Bohra communities, it has been subject to greater lexical influence by Arabic and Persian and is written in the Arabic script.

Kutchi is often referred to as a dialect of Gujarati, but most linguists consider it closer to Sindhi. In addition, a mixture between Sindhi, Gujarati, and Kutchi called Memoni is related to Gujarati, albeit distantly.

Furthermore, words used by the native languages of areas where the Gujarati people have become a diaspora community, such as East Africa (Swahili), have become loanwords in local dialects of Gujarati.

Writing system

Similar to other Nâgarî writing systems, the Gujarati script is an abugida. It is used to write the Gujarati and Kutchi languages.

It is a variant of Devanâgarî script differentiated by the loss of the characteristic horizontal line running above the letters and by a small number of modifications in the remaining characters.

Gujarati and closely related languages, including Kutchi and Parkari Koli, can be written in the Arabic or Persian scripts. This is traditionally done by many in Gujarat's Kutch district.

GUJARATI LITERATURE

The history of Gujarati literature may be traced to 1000 AD, and this literature has flourished since then to the present. It is unique in having almost no patronage from a ruling dynasty, other than its composers.

Gujarat Vidhya Sabha, Gujarat Sahitya Sabha, Gujarat Sahitya Akademi and Gujarati Sahitya Parishad are Gujarat-based literary institutions promoting the Gujarati literature.

History

Such factors as the policies of the rulers, the living style of the people, and the worldwide influence on society are important for any literature to flourish. In Gujarat, due to the development of trade and commerce, the religious influence of Jainism as well as Hinduism, and also due to the safety and encouragement of rulers like Chaulukya (Solanki) and Vaghela Rajputs, literary activities were in full force from the 11th century.

- Gujarati literature
- Early literature (up to 1450 AD)
- Prâg-Narsinh Yug (1000 AD to 1450 AD)
- Râsa Yug
- Medieval literature (1450 AD – 1850 AD)
- Narsinh Yug (1450 AD to 1850 AD)
- Bhakti Yug
- SaguG☐ Bhakti Yug
- NirguG☐ Bhakti Yug
- Modern literature (1850 AD to date)
- Sudhârak Yug or Narmad Yug
- PaG☐it Yug or Govardhan Yug (1885–1915 AD)
- Gandhi Yug (1915–1945 AD)
- Anu-Ghandhi Yug (1940–1955 AD)
- Âdhunik Yug (1955–1985 AD)
- Anu-Âdunik Yug

Literature in Gujarati is sometimes also classified into two broad categories, namely poetry and prose, the former savouring and basking in its long lineage, dating back to the 6th century. Poetry as a perception was a medium for expressing religious beliefs and judgements, a stronghold of medieval Indian times. In this context of gradual evolution, the history of Gujarati literature is generally classed into three broad periods, consisting of the Early period (up to c. 1450 AD), the Middle period (1450 to 1850 AD) and the Modern period (1850 AD. onwards). However, Gujarati literature and its tremendous maturation and proficiency in contributing to culture is retraced back to Gujarat Sultanate days (referring to the Muzaffarid dynasty, which had provided the sultans of Gujarat in western India from 1391 to 1583).

Gujarati literature is divided mainly into three eras or *Yugas*; the early, medieval and modern, with these eras being further subdivided.

Early literature

Pre-Narsinh Era (1000 AD to 1450 AD)

The Jain monk and scholar Hemacandrâcârya Suri was one of the earliest scholars of Prakrit and Apabhramsha grammars. He had penned a formal set of 'grammarian principles' as the harbinger of the Gujarati language during the reign of the Chaulukyaking Jayasimha Siddharaja of Anhilwara. This treatise formed the cornerstone of Apabhramsa grammar in the Gujarati language, establishing a language from a combination of corrupted forms of languages like Sanskrit and Ardhamagadhi. He authored *Kavyanushasana* (Poetics), a handbook or manual of poetry, *Siddha-haima-shabdanushasana* on Prakrit and Apabhramsha grammars, and *Desinamamala*, a list of words of local origin.

It is generally accepted by historians and researchers in literary genres in Gujarati literature that the earliest writings in this very ancient language were by Jaina authors. These were composed in the form of Râsas, Phâgus and Vilâsas. Râsas were long poems which were essentially heroic, romantic or narrative in nature. Úâlîbhadra Sûri's *Bharateúvara Bâhubalî râsa* (1185 AD), Vijayasena's *Revantagiri-râsa* (1235 AD), Ambadeva's *Samararasa* (1315 AD) and Vinayaprabha's *Gautama Svâmi râsa* (1356 AD) are the most illustrious examples of this form of literature in Gujarati. The chief sbjects of Rasas were descriptions of nature, erotic depictions of seasons, Jain Acharyas and Tirthankaras, biographies of historic characters. The collections of these Rasas are currently preserved in Jain libraries of Patan, Ahmedabad, Jaisalmer and Khambhat.

The phâgus are poems that pictured the blissful and cheery nature of the spring festival (Vasanta). They were written by Jain monks but are not centred on religion. Râjasekhara's *Neminatha-phagu* (1344 AD) and unknown poet's *Vasanta-vilâsa* (1350 AD) are instances of such texts. *Vasantavilasa* had 84 stanzas and is similar to a phagu of the same name so it is possible that both are written by the same person.

Other notable prabandha or narrative poems of this period include Úrîdhara's *RaGāmalla Chhanda* (1398 AD), Merutunga's *Prabandhachintamani*, Padmanâbha's *Kânha*

Among non-Jain writers of the time, Asait Thakar is considered as a major contributor who wrote around 360 *vesha* (lit. dress) of Bhavai. He is credited with bringing theatre to the Gujarati literature. Abdur Raheman, who wrote *Sandeshkarash*, is considered as the first Muslim writer of Gujarati literature.

Due to flourishing trade and commerce in Ahmedabad and Khambat (Cambay), entertainment activities started to develop, and the Jain saints, story-tellers, puppet shows, and Bhavai (dramas) also revived literature.

Medieval literature

During this period, the poetry dominated the literary activities. As Rasas written by Jain monks were a type of narrative poetry, Akhyanas are considered as their literary descendants which reached their glory in this period. Garbo and Garbi poetry associated with dance were developed as well as phagu and Barmasi genres depicting seasons. The types of *pada: prabhatiya, dhol, kafi* and *chabkha* were created. So the singable poetry, a tradition inherited from *Apabhramsa*, developed and dominated in the period.

Narsinh Era (1450 AD – 1850 AD)

During the 15th century, Gujarati literature had come under the tremendous sway of the Bhakti movement, a popular cultural movement to liberate religion from entrenched priesthood. Narsinh Mehta (15th century) was the foremost poet of this era. His poems delineated a very saintly and mystical sense and bore an intense reflection of the philosophy of Advaita. Narsinh Mehta's *Govind Gaman, Surat Sangram, Sudama Charitra* and *Sringaramala* are illustrations of this devotional poetry. Due to his poetic style, the works of contemporary and early poets were obscured.

Bhakti Era (15th–19th century)

During this age, Jain and Hindu poets produced Gujarat literature in abundance. The prose and poetry created were aimed to encourage religion and worship. Hindu texts such as Gita, Mahabharata, Vedas, and Bhagwata became popular. There were also creations of prayers, Jain history, etc. During this period of the influence of the Bhakti Movement on Gujarati literature, the Ramayana, the Bhagavad Gita, the Yogavashistha and the Panchatantra were all translated into Gujarati. This period also experienced the colossal Puranic revival, which led to the rapid growth and maturation of devotional poetry in Gujarati literature. This era is divided into two traditions, Sagun Bhakti tradition and Nirgun Bhakti tradition.

Sagun Bhakti tradition

In this tradition, the God is worshiped in physical form, having some form and virtues like Rama and Krishna. Narsinh Mehta, Meera, and Dayaram were foremost contributors of this tradition.

Meera supplied many *Pada* (Verse). Premanand Bhatt was

a prolific poet and number of folklore are about him. He is credited with writing 47 works but scholars accredits only 27 works to him. He chiefly authored works on Narsinh Mehta, Bhagvat and Mahabharata. His notable works are *Okha Harana, Nalakhyana, Abhimanyu Akhyana, Dasham Skandha* and *Sudama Charitra.*

Shamal Bhatt was an extremely creative and productive poet who gave birth to unforgettable works like *Padmavati, Batris Putli, Nanda Batrisi, Sinhasan Batrisi* and *Madana Mohan* in Gujarati verse writing. His works also depicts strong female characters compared to contemporary works for the first time in Gujarati literature.Dayaram (1767–1852) had given rise to religious, ethical and romantic lyrics referred to as Garbi. His most authoritative works comprise *Bhakti Poshan, Rasik Vallabh*and *Ajamel Akhyan.* His death is considered as the end of medieval period of Gujarati literature. The "Ramayana" was authored by Giridhara in Gujarati during the middle of the 19th century. Parmanand, Brahmanand, Vallabha, Haridas, Ranchhod and Divali Bai were other authoritative 'saint poets' from this period of poetry predomination in Gujarati literature.

Nirgun Bhakti tradition

The God has no physical form in this tradition.

Narsinh Mehta and Akho were the foremost contributors of this tradition. His works depicts contemporary society, philosophy, behaviour and humour. Akho's *Akhe Gita, Chittavichar Samvad* and *Anubhav Bindu* have always been illustrated as being emphatic compositions on the Vedanta. Yet another poet, Mandana, had authored works like *Prabodha Battrisi, Ramayan* and *Rupmangal Katha.* Other contributors are Kabir-Panthi poets, Dhira Bhagat, Bhoja Bhagat, Bapusaheb Gaikwad, and Pritam.

Others

Poets from the Swaminarayan sect such as Sahajanand Swami, Brahmanand Swami, Premanand Swami and

Nishkulanand Swami also contributed immensely. Their works were focused on morality, devotion and reclusion. Parsi poets also entered Gujarati literature during this period. Their notable works are translation of Parsi religious literature in Gujarati. Eravad Rustom Peshot is considered as the first Parsi Gujarati poet who wrote biographies such as *Zarthost-nameh, Siyavaksha-nameh, Viraf-nameh* and *Aspandiar-nameh.*

Modern literature (1850 AD – present)

With the colonial British Government and the new technology of printing and press, education in the English language began. The new age brought many newspapers and magazines, which spread awareness in society. Because of this, there was much more literature, and it included forms other than the ancient religious style of poetry. The creations reflect social welfare, criticism, plays, new-age thinking, worship of the country, the values of life, etc. This period is subdivided into following eras: Reformist Era or Narmad Era, Scholar Era or Govardhan Era, Gandhi Era, Post-Gandhi Era, Modern Era and Postmodern Era.

Reformist Era or Narmad Era (1850–1885 AD)

From the middle of 19th century, Gujarati, like other regional Indian languages, came under strong western influence, precisely due to colonial residence and colonial reign. Western education and culture started to influence local culture and the awareness was spread about pervasive customs of Hindu society. Two sections in society emerged: conservative following traditional customs as a cultural duty and liberal which believed in opposition and end of social pervasive customs and injustice So Prarthana Samaj, Arya Samaj, Theosophical Society were established which wanted to reform society through religion while other reformers believed in non-religious way of reform. Social reform was a central subjects in works of this era. Narmad, Govardhanram Tripathi and Gatubhai Gopilal Dhruv advocated reform through religion while Ramanbhai Nilkanth, Narsinhrao Divetia and Kant advocated non-religious way.

Dalpatram (1820–1898) and Narmad (1833–1886) are the trailblazers of modern Gujarati literature. Dalpatram's *Venacharitra* portrays his command over hilarity and wittiness. He contributed in prose and poetry. His prose works include plays, essays and other works such as *Laxminatak, Mithyabhiman, Streesambhashan, Tarkikbodh, Daivagnadarpan* and *Bhootnibandh*. His poetry include *Farbasvilas, Farbasvirah, Dalpatpingal* and *Hope Vachanmala*. Modern studies of Gujarat and its language began with the British administrator Alexander Kinlock Forbes shortly after the British occupation of the region. Alexander Forbes carried out an extensive investigation of Gujarati culture and literature over the previous thousand years and amassed a large collection of manuscripts. An organisation named after him, called the Farbas Gujarati Sabha, dedicates itself to the preservation and promotion of Gujarati literature and language and history from its headquarters in Mumbai. The first Gujarati dictionary, known as *Narmakosh*, was composed and compiled by Narmad; it is essentially a history of the world, and also an authority on poetics. He moved away from the subjects of medieval literature and wrote on freedom, nationalism, nature and romance. He attempted many varieties of poetry and smoothly adapted English verses into Gujarati. He wrote the first autobiography *Mari Hakikat* of Gujarati literature. He also wrote essays and plays. His *Rukmini Haran* and *Virasinh* are considered by scholars to be masterpiece compendia of poems.

Navalram Pandya pioneered criticism in Gujarati. The other notable works in Gujarati literature in this era are Bholanath Sarabhai's *Ishvara Prarthanamala* (1872), Navalram Pandya's *Bhatt nu Bhopalu* (1867) and *Veermati* (1869), and Nandshankar Mehta's *Karan Ghelo* (1866), which was the first original novel of Gujarati literature.

Ranchhodlal Udayaram Dave (1837–1923) is respected as the groundbreaker and trailblazer in the art of play-writing in Gujarati with his *Lalita Dukh Darsak* play. Other significant dramatists were Dalpatram, Narmad and Navalram.

Parsi writers of the era include Behramji Malabari who first authored original works in standardised Gujarati. Parsi authors wrote large number of works in Parsi Gujarati and standard Gujarati dialects as well as translated novels from English and French literature. They are credited with establishment of Gujarati theatre.

Scholar Era or Govardhan Era (1885–1915 AD)

Pandit means 'a scholar' in Gujarati. During this era, the scholarly writing developed gradually, hence it in know by *Pandit era*. The era is considered by Dhirubhai Thaker as a golden era of Gujarati literature when poetry, play, essays and biography reached its zenith. The writers of this era were authoring under the influence of westernisation and social reforms. In politics, it was a period of rise of Indian independence movement, established western education system and western study of ancient religious literature and cultural renaissance. The foreign literature had started influencing local literature in India and people were exposed to the outer influence. The writers of this era also had a reformative bent of mind, but they paid more attention towards literary accomplishments. Their fundamental belief was that the literature is not an art that anybody can attempt to write whatever comes to mind, but it is a creative art which demands seriousness and responsibility.

Govardhanram Tripathi is the major novelists of era whose celebrated classic novel is *Saraswatichandra*.

The work of others includes Narsinhrao Divetia's "Smarana Samhita", "Kusumamala", "Hridayavina", "Nupur Jhankar" and "Buddha Charit"; Manishankar Ratanji Bhatt or Kavi Kant's "Purvalap" ('Devayani', 'Atijnana', 'Vasanta Vijay' and 'Chakravak Mithuna') and Balwantray Thakore's "Bhanakar". Nhanalal was another important poet of this period in Gujarati literature, who had outshone incredibly in his *"Apadya Gadya"* or rhyming prose. Nhanalal's recognition and reputation is based on two poetic compilations, namely "Vasantotsava" (1898) and "Chitradarshan" (1921), an epic referred to as "Kuruksetra", and numerous plays like "Indukumar", "Jayajayant", "Vishva Gita", "Sanghamitra" and "Jagat Prerana".

Gandhi Era (1915–1945 AD)

Mahatma Gandhi

The Pandit Era came to an end in 1914, when the First World War broke out. Mahatma Gandhi, with his weapon of Satyagraha(Friendly passive resistance) tried and tested in South Africa. Gandhiji left Africa and arrived in early January 1915. With penetrating insight he observed first hand the socio-economic and political conditions obtaining in India and thought about every questions related to life. After Gandhi's arrival on the Indian scene, the literary climate of Gujarat, which was the hub of all Gandhi's socio-political activities, underwent a rapid change. Gandhi started editing *Navajivan*, a weekly periodical, and spread his thoughts and ideology.

During this period, Mahatma Gandhi and Gujarat Vidyapith became the nerve-centre of all literary activities, where new values emerged and more emphasis was given to Gandhian values, Indianisation and simplification. Novels, short stories, diaries, letters, plays, essays, criticisms, biographies, travel books and all kinds of prose began to flood Gujarati literature.

Gandhi, Ramnarayan Pathak, Kanaiyalal Munshi or K. M. Munshi, Swami Anand, Umashankar Joshi, Sundaram, Jhaverchand Meghani, Pannalal Patel, Jyotindra Dave, Chandravadan Mehta, Zinabhai Desai ("Snehrashmi"), Vaid Mohanlal Chunilal Dhami, Manubhai Pancholi ("Darshak"), and Ishwar Petlikar are the main contributors of this age.

Modern Gujarati prose was ushered in with a bang by Narmad, but K.M. Munshi and, of course, the legend and nationalist himself, Mahatma Gandhi, gave it prominence in this age. Gandhi's autobiography, *An Autobiography of My Experiments with Truth ((Gujarâtî "" " " ""))*, *Satyagraha in South Africa* about his struggle there, *Hind Swaraj or Indian Home Rule*, a political pamphlet, and a paraphrase in Gujarati of John Ruskin's *Unto The Last* are his most well-known works. This last essay sets out his programme on economics. He wrote extensively on vegetarianism, diet and health, religion, social reforms, etc. Gandhi usually wrote in Gujarati, though he also revised the Hindi and English translations of his books.

Gandhi was a prolific writer. For decades he edited several newspapers including *Harijan* in Gujarati, Hindi and English; *Indian Opinion* while in South Africa and, *Young India*, in English, and "Navajivan", a Gujarati monthly, on his return to India. Later, "Navajivan" was published in Hindi. He wrote letters almost every day to individuals and newspapers.

During the 1940s, there could be witnessed a rise in communistic poetry and this inspired a movement for progressive literature in Gujarati too. Meghani, Bhogilal Gandhi, Swapnastha and others began to preach class conflict and hatred of religion through their writings. K.M. Munshi is deemed one of the most multi-talented and flexible and looming literary figures of Gujarati literature of contemporary times. K.M. Munshi's voluminous works include dramas, essays, short stories and novels. His famous novels are included in the list of "Patan ni Prabhuta", "Gujarat no Nath", "Jay Somnath" (1940), "Prithvi Vallabh", "Bhagavan Parshuram" (1946) and "Tapasvini" (1957).

Indeed, after the rise of Mahatma Gandhi's prominence in a steadily strengthening struggle for independence and social equality, a great volume of poetry, written by poets like Umashankar, Sundaram, Shesh, Snehrashmi and Betai, amongst others, centred on the existing social order, the struggle for independence and the travails of Mahatma Gandhi himself. Highly inspired by Rabindranath Tagore's dialogue poems, Umashankar Joshi enriched the existing Gujrati literature by penning in the same manner. Two such poems are his "Prachina" and "Mahaprasthan". For his poem "Nishith", he received the Jnanpith Award in 1967. Pannalal Patel received the Jnanpith Award in 1985 for his novel "Maanavi Ni Bhavaai".

The Gujarati novel was also made a household name by G.G. Joshi ('Dhumketu'), Chunilal V. Shah, Gunvantrai Acharya, Jhaverchand Meghani, Pannalal Patel and Manubhai Pancholi.

Significant dramatists of this age are Chandravadan Mehta, Umashankar Joshi, Jayanti Dalal and Chunilal Madia.

Amongst the important essayists, citation can be made of Kaka Kalelkar, Ratilal Trivedi, Lilavati Munshi, Jyotindra Dave, Ramnarayan Pathak.

Post-Ghandhi Era (1940–1955 AD)

In this era there is a dominance of poetry. The main contributors of this age are Niranjan Bhagat, Rajendra Shah, Venibhai Purohit, Prahlad Parekh and Balmukund Dave. Rajendra Shah won the Jnanpith—the Indian government's most prestigious literary prize—for the year 2001. The judges noted, "his intensity of emotion and innovation in form and expression which set him apart as a poet of great significance. The mystical tone of his poetry stems from the tradition of great medieval masters like Kabir, Narsinh Mehta and literary giants like them". He authored more than 20 collections of poems and songs, mainly on the themes of the beauty of nature, and about the everyday lives of indigenous peoples and fisherfolk communities. In his poems using Sanskrit metrics, he was influenced by Rabindranath Tagore. He was one of the giants of the post Gandhi-era, called 'Anu-Gandhi Yug' in Gujarati literature.

Modern Era (1955–1985 AD)

Suresh Joshi

Post-independence Gujarati poetry displays a higher form of subjectivity and explores newer philosophies and lines of thought and imagery. The poems became more subjective and brutal, discarding old imageries and symbols and replacing them with new ideas. Prominent Gujarati poets of the post-independence era include critically acclaimed poets like Suresh Joshi, Gulam Mohamed Sheikh, Harindra Dave, Manoj Khanderia, Chinu Modi, Nalin Raval and Adil Mansuri, among others.

Post-independence prose literature in Gujarati had two distinct trends, traditional and modern. The former dealt more with ethical values and its main writers were Gulabdas Broker, Mansukhlal Jhaveri, Vishnuprasad Trivedi and others. Existentialism, surrealism and symbolism influenced the latter. The modernists also wanted to do away with moral values and religious beliefs. Eminent writers of this trend comprise Niranjan Bhagat, Chandrakant Bakshi, Suresh Joshi, Madhu Rye, Raghuveer Chaudhari, Dhiruben Patel, Saroj Pathak, and others. There was also a noticeable segment of Popular writers like Vithal Pandya, Sarang Barot, Dinkar Joshi, Harkisan Mehta and Ashwinee Bhatt whose novels found a place in the hearts of common people. Their novels reached every corner of Gujarat and also to vast Gujarati readers outside Gujarat through newspapers and magazines. Gujarati prose has recorded growth and literary feats quite rapidly in less than two hundred years and now can be counted among the front benchers in Indian literature.

Postmodern Era (1985 – present)

Bhagwatikumar Sharma, Vinesh Antani, Dhruv Bhatt, Yogesh Joshi, Bindu Bhatt, Kanji Patel brought freshness in narration in novels. Same can be said for Bholabhai Patel, Manilal H. Patel, Anil Joshi for essays. Some new poets have also given significant literary work including Sanju Vala, Rajesh Vyas 'Miskin', Ankit Trivedi, Rajesh Vankar, Anil Chavda, Bhavesh Bhatt, Ashok Chavda, Kiransinh Chauhan, Neerav Patel and many others.

In this age, the other outstanding themes are Dalit literature and 'feminist literature'. Modern poetry continued to take its roots deep.

Literary forms

- Akhyana (narrative poetry)
- Rasa
- Prabandha
- Barmasi

- Pada (verse)
- Padya-Vaarta
- Chhappa
- Khand-Kavya
- Bhavai
- Natak (play)
- Navalkatha (novel)
- Navlika (Novella)
- Tunki Varta (short story)
- Urmi-Kavita (lyric)
- Ghazal
- Aatma-Katha (autobiography)
- Jivan-Charitra (biography)
- Nibandh (essay)
- Fagu (lyrical poetry)
- Children's literature

Firsts

- The printing was introduced in Gujarati in 1812. The first printed book published was the Gujarati translation of *Dabestan-e Mazaheb* prepared and printed by Parsi priest Fardunjee Marzban in 1815.

- 1822, first Gujarati newspaper: *Mumbai Samachar*, the oldest newspaper in India still in circulation.

- 1840s, personal diary composition: *Nityanondh*, Durgaram Mehta.

- 1845, first modern Gujarati poem: *Bapani Piparu* (Father's Pipar Tree), Dalpatram

- 1851, first essay: Mandali Malvathi Thata Labh, Narmadashankar Dave

- 1866, first original novel: *KaraG⌐Ghelo*, Nandshankar Mehta.

- 1866, first social novel: *Sasu Vahu ni Ladai*, Mahipatram Rupram Nilkanth

- 1866, first autobiography: *Mârî Hakîkat*, Narmadashankar Dave.

- 1900, first original short story: *Shantidas*, Ambalal Desai.

5

Geography and Flora and Fauna

GEOGRAPHY

Gujarat borders Pakistan's Tharparkar, Badin and Thatta districts of Sindh province to the northwest, is bounded by the Arabian Sea to the southwest, the state of Rajasthan to the northeast, Madhya Pradesh to the east, and by Maharashtra, Union territories of Diu, Daman, Dadra and Nagar Haveli to the south. Historically, the north was known as Anarta, the Kathiawar peninsula, "Saurastra", and the south as "Lata". Gujarat was also known as Pratichya and Varuna. The Arabian Sea makes up the state's western coast. The capital, Gandhinagar is a planned city. Gujarat has an area of 75,686 sq mi (196,030 km) with the longest coast line(24% of Indian sea coast) 1,600 kilometres (990 mi), dotted with 41 ports: one major, 11 intermediate and 29 minor.

The Sabarmati is the largest river in Gujarat followed by the Tapi, although the Narmada covers the longest distance in its passage through the state. The Sardar Sarovar Project is built on the Narmada River, one of the major rivers of peninsular India with a length of around 1,312 kilometres (815 mi). It is one of only three rivers in peninsular India that run from east to west – the others being the Tapi River and the Mahi River. A riverfront project has been built on the Sabarmati River.

Sardar Sarovar Project, Gujarat, partially completed (up to E.L.121.92 m)

Rann of Kutch

The Rann of Kutch is a seasonally marshy saline clay desert located in the Thar Desert biogeographic region in between the province of Sindh and the state of Gujarat. Situated 8 kilometres (5.0 mi) from the village of Kharaghoda in the Surendranagar District and Pakistan's Sindh province. The name "Rann" comes from the Gujarati word rann (") meaning "desert".

DISTRICTS OF GUJARAT

The detail analysis of Population Census 2011 published by Govt. of India for Gujarat state reveal that population of Gujarat has increased by 19.28% in this decade compared (2001-2011) to past decade (1991-2001). The density of Gujarat state in the current decade is 798 per sq mile.

- Gujarat is an State of India with population of Approximate 6.04 Crores.
- The population of Gujarat state is 60,439,692.
- The density of Gujarat state is 308 per sq km.

- Gujarat State is spread over 196,244 Sq Km.

BEACHES

Ahmedpur Mandvi Beach - Ahmedpur Mandvi Beach is situated on the coastline of the state of Gujarat and is one of the finest beaches in India. It is in Ahmedpur Mandvi, close to Union Territory Diu.

Mandvi Beach - Kutch - Mandvi Wind Farms Beach and Wind-mills, which line the horizon of Mandvi, offer views from the Mandvi sea-beach. The Wind mills projects running in this beach was Asia's 1st Wind-Mills Projects in 1983.

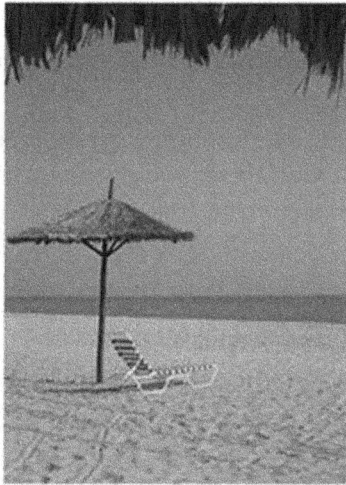

Mandvi Beach, Kutch

Chorwad Beach - Chorwad Beach of Gujarat is another beach situated on the west coast of India. It is situated at a distance of 66 km from Junagadh. Chorwad has a high potential of attracting both domestic as well as international tourists. The beach consists of rocky hills and presents an opportunity for boat rides.

Diu Beach - Diu beach is situated off the Saurashtra coast and is connected to the state of Gujarat via a causeway. Diu is a secluded island and does not have much population.

Gopnath Beach - Gopnath Beach is situated in the Bhavnagar district of Gujarat. It comes into Talaja Taluka. It is located on the coast of the Gulf of Kambhat, at a distance of 75 km from the city of Bhavnagar. and 22 km. away from Talaja. The Fort of the King of Gohilvad is situated in Gopnath.

Kutch Mandvi Beach — Kutch Mandvi is an important beach in Gujarat, situated at Mandvi. Mandvi is the historic port town of Maharao of Kutch, located at a distance of 75 km from Bhuj. Kutch Mandvi was once inhabited by the Maharao of Kutch and was an important seaport.

Umbergam Beach - Umargam is about 6 km from Umargam Road railway station on Mumbai-Surat rail section . This region was a part of Thane district prior to the creation of Gujarat in 1960.

Umargam is situated on the southern bank of Nargol creek. It was a small village about two centuries ago, serving as a transit point for exporting marine produce from the fishing port Nargol on the Northern Bank of the creek.

Tithal Beach (Valsad) Tithal beach 5 km from Valsad.

FLORA AND FAUNA

Gujarat is rich in its store of flora and fauna. The geography of Gujarat boasts of having a wide variety of flora and fauna which are spread throughout its length and breadth.

In Gujarat, one can find as many as 500 varieties of mammals, more than 2000 species of birds, a wide range of insects, fishes, amphibians, reptiles, etc. - this aspect, indeed, makes Gujarat rich in terms of flora and fauna.

Some of the important mammals found in Gujarat are:

- black bucks
- nilgai
- chitals
- wild boar

- four horned antelope
- hyenas
- rusty spotted cats, etc.

A large number of other animals like snakes, lizards, crocodiles, scorpions, bees, silkworm, Lac insect, etc., are found in the forest of Gujarat. Some of the dangerous breed of animals are also found in forests of Gujarat, such as mosquitoes and locusts which are fatal both for mankind and animals.

The flora and fauna of Gujarat is incomplete without a reference to the birds. Many kinds of birds are found here, such as:

- peacock
- parrots
- pheasants
- geese ducks
- cranes, etc.

Flora in Gujarat include a wide variety of vegetation. A wide range of climatic condition facilitates the prevalence of many types of flora. In Gujarat, we find more than 400 species of flora. The flora in Gujarat include one of the largest dry deciduous forests in the western region of India, including trees like:

- teak
- Boswellia serrata
- Anogeissus latifolia
- Diospyros, etc.

Owing to the arid climate, the flora and fauna of Gujarat also possess a wide range of xerophytic vegetation. This kind of vegetation include:

- Acacia arabica
- Acacia leucophloea
- Capparis ophylla

• Zizyphus mauratiana, etc.

Therefore, as it is evident, Gujarat has an enormous store of flora and fauna. In fact, it has one of the major forests in India, i.e. the Gir Forest which has the highest number of Asian lions. Incredible!

CONSERVING GUJARAT'S FLORA & FAUNA!

If you have visited Gir since the forest opened for tourists after the monsoon, it would have been difficult to miss the new kids on the block. This season has been marked by the birth of 90 cubs, which is a rise of 20% as compared to last year. "It was the young Simbas who hogged the limelight" is how the Times of India described the euphoria as the forest reopened.

But the good news does not end here. There is a story within this story, which makes one even more proud of Gujarat and its efforts to conserve the Asiatic Lion. Every season 75 cubs are born but this time the higher number is attributed to the increase in the lioness population. The female-male ratio stands significantly improved- from 76 lions and 100 lionesses, the number now stands at 97 lions and 162 lionesses.

A recent study revealed that Asiatic lion cubs survive much better in Gujarat's Gir forests as compared to Africa. The study revealed that 56% of cubs in Asia survive beyond three years, the age when the cub moves out of its pride. In contrast, the number of African lions that live beyond two years is 20%!

The census of lions in 2010 stated that the population of Asiatic lions in Gir has grown by 13% over a period of 5 years, taking the total to 411. Usually the growth rate stands between 5 to 7% but the latest figures indicated a sharp surge. That time, Shri Narendra Modi had called it Gujarat's gift to the world on the state's golden jubilee.

Cherishing our nature, conserving our wildlife

The success at Gir is just one of the countless examples of the Gujarat Government to preserve the flora and fauna of the state. This is an issue about which Shri Modi is extremely passionate. He has correctly written that conserving our environment and nature has been a part of our culture for ages. He has always called for living in harmony with Mother Nature without causing any harm to our surroundings.

Another example of an effort to preserve our fauna is the Blackbuck National Park, which has been hailed as a unique model of wildlife conservation. The National Park, which is in Velavadar is one of the few sites where Blackbucks are found in such large numbers and the number of Blackbucks have constantly risen due to favourable conditions in the park. The Park is home to rich biodiversity, which is made possible due to combined efforts of the park authorities and the local people.

Authorities say they have not heard of a single case of poaching in the last ten years! This again shows, with determined efforts and people's participation, a lot is possible.

Significant Rise in Gujarat's Mangrove Cover

In February this year, it came out that India witnessed a 23.34 sqkm increase in its mangrove cover between 2009 and 2011 thanks to the efforts of none other than Gujarat! A report by the Forest Survey of India commended Gujarat's role in planting mangroves. Mangroves are regarded as productive wetlands and are home to many flora and faunal species, many of which are critically endangered.

Home to a quarter of the nation's mangroves covering 1046 sqkm, Gujarat is home to the second highest mangrove cover after West Bengal. Having the nation's longest coastline, Gujarat is an ideal atmosphere for mangroves to flourish.

To restore this precious ecosystem the Gujarat Ecology Commission launched a restoration project with Community Based Management. This not only included mangrove plantation but also spreading awareness. In an extremely commendable move, the Gujarat Government allotted Rs. 15.21 crore in the 2011-2012 budget for enhancing the mangrove cover.

Under Shri Modi's guidance, the state Government has taken initiatives to increase tree cover in cities. In this regard special mention must be made about Gandhinagar, which was recently hailed as the Tree Capital of India. Latest figures show that 54% of the city is under green cover, making it 416 trees for every 100 people in the city. At a time when urbanization puts the growth of trees under threat, Gandhinagar is a perfect point of inspiration.

The total forest area has gone up from 1291 (thousand hectares) in 2001 to 1833 (thousand hectares) in 2011. In 2003 there were 25.1 crore trees outside the forest cover and in 2009 the number went up to 26.9 crore. Shri Modi intends to take this number further up to 35 crore over the next decade.

Van Mahotsavs

This is the brainchild of Shri Modi and examples his dynamism and determination towards preserving our forests. Shri Modi enhanced public participation in the planting of trees. Since 2005, Van Mahotsavs has spread into various parts of Gujarat, creating a mass movement for a greener Gujarat.

The 2012 Van Mahotsav commenced from Mangadh, a beautiful village in Panchmahal, which is home to Tribal heroes of Gujarat who waged a war against Colonial rulers in 1913 and lost their lives at the hands of colonial brutality! Shri Modi inaugurated Smriti Van as a tribute to these martyrs.

CLIMATE

The climate of Gujarat is moist in the southern districts and dry in the northern region. The Arabian sea and the Gulf of Cambay reduce the temperature and render the climate more pleasant and healthy. The year can be divided into: the winter season from November to February, the hot season from March to May, the south-west monsoon season from June to September and the intervening month of October.

The average rainfall in Gujarat varies from 33 to 152 cms. The southern region of the state has an average rainfall ranging from 76 to 152 cms, Dangs district having the highest average of about 190 cms. The northern districts have a rainfall varying from 51 to 102 cms. The rainfall in the southern highlands of Saurashtra and the Gulf of Cambay is approximately 63 cms while the other parts of Saurashtra have a rainfall less than 63 cms.

The semi-desert area of Kutch has a very low average rainfall. Certain areas in Ahmedabad, Mehsana, Banaskantha, Panchmahals, Surendranagar, Jamnagar and Kutch districts face chronic scarcity conditions for want of adequate rains.

As the Tropic of Cancer passes through the northern border of Gujarat, the state has an intensely hot or cold climate. But the Arabian sea and the Gulf of Cambay in the west and the forest covered hills in the east soften the rigors of climatic extremes.

NATURAL FEATURES

The relief is low in the most parts of the state and involves diverse climate conditions. The winters are mild, pleasant, and dry with average daytime temperatures around 83F(29C) and nights around 83F(29C) The summers are extremely hot and dry with day temperatures around 115F(46C) and at night no lower than 83F(29C) The time just before the monsoon the temperature are similar to above but now there is high humidity which makes the air feel hotter. Relief comes when the monsoon season starts around in mid June.

The day temperatures are lower to around 100F(38C) but humidity is very high and nights are around 83F(29C) Most of the rainfall occurs in this season. Though mostly dry, it is desertic in the north-west, and wet in the southern districts due to heavy monsoon season.

With the construction of Sardar Sarovar on Narmada River, a result of the largest dam in India, irrigation facilities have improved immensely, with water being provided to the most dry areas of Kutch and Saurashtra through a 550 km long canal. With the Gulf of Kutch and the Gulf of Cambay, Gujarat has about 1600 km of coastline, which is the longest coastline of all Indian states.

RIVERS

The major rivers flowing through the state include the Narmada, Sabarmati, and Mahi in central and northern Gujarat; Mithi, Khari, Bhadar, Shetrunji and Bhogavo in Saurashtra; Narmada, Tapi, Purna, Ambika, Auranga and Damanganga in the southern part of the state.

The Banas in the north, originating in the Siranva hill in Sirohi in Rajasthan, flows by the foot hills of Abu and disappears in the desert. The Saraswati takes its birth at Koteshvar near Ambaji, flows by Siddhpur and Patan and merges into the desert.

The Sabarmati, one of the biggest rivers of north Gujarat, originates from the Dhebar lake in Rajasthan and flows towards the Gulf of Cambay. The Hathmati, the Vatrak, the Mazam, the Meshvo, the Shedhi, the Khari and the other rivulets join it.

The three "virgin" rivers of the north and the Sabarmati with its tributaries are the daughters of the Aravalli ranges, while the Mahi and the Narmada with their families originate from Madhya Pradesh, the former in the big lake near Amzara and the latter in the Amarkantak. The Mahi is joined by the Bhadar, the Anas, the Panam and the Meshri. The Narmada one of the biggest and holiest river along with the only tributary, the Karjan, meets the sea, about 16km from Broach.

The Tapi takes its birth in the Satpura ranges near Betwa and enters Gujarat at Kakarapar. It flows around Surat and Rander and falls into the sea.

The Mindhola, the Purna, the Ambika, the Vanki, the Auranga, the Vapi, the Par, the Kolak and the Damanganga are the rivers of south Gujarat, which originate in the Sahyadri.

Most of the rivers of Saurashtra and Kutch dry up in the summer. The river which originate in the central Saurashtra in the Chotila range flow to the south into the desert of Kutch. Only the Aji, the Machhu and the Brahmani are northward flowing rivers. The rivers originating in the Girnar and the Gir namely the Ojhat, the Kamb, the Surekh, the Somal, the Sangwada, the Hirani, the Kpila and the Saraswati flow into the sea. The Saraswati near the Somnath and the Vastu are sacred rivers.

Though Kutch has many rivers, they are small and do not have much water. Those flowing in the north disappear in the desert, while those flowing in other directions join the sea. The Khari flowing by Bhuj meets the desert and the Magh and the Tara empty their waters in the Gulf of Cambay. The Rudramata has been bunded for irrigation, providing the only irrigation project in Kutch.

DAMS

A number of large dams has been built in Gujarat over last 30-35 years, many of them partly funded by the World Bank. These dams were built with the promise of irrigation, power generation, enhanced food production and other benefits. The major Dams flowing through the state include the Narmada River, Tapi, Mahi, Damanganaga, Dantiwada- Sipu Dams, Sabarmati, Indrasee Hatmati, Wanakbori.

MOUNTAINS

Gujarat's mountains are rich in scenic beauty and have been closely associated with religious and historical currents of Gujarat's life. The northern and the eastern borders are made up of mountains which are themselves either the tails or offshoots of outside ranges like the Aravallis, the Vindhyas, the Satpuras and the Sahyadris. Saurashtra contains two parallel ranges, one stretching from east to west and the other from north-east to south-west. The tracts of saline land of Kutch have three mountain ranges.

The Aravalli which is the most ancient mountain range in Gujarat lies largely in Rajasthan and enters Gujarat at Abu and zigzagging up to the Pavagadh merges into the Vindhyas. The Taranga lies on the line from Mehsana to Visnagar.

The Arasur branch of the Aravalli goes in the direction of Danta, Khedbrahma, Idar and Shamlaji and joins the Vindhyas. The Satpura tail lies between the Narmada and the Tapi with Rajpipla hills. The ranges of the Sahyadri lie across the Tapi with the highest rainfall and the densest forest in the state. The Saler Muler and the Parner form part of the Sahyadri range.

The rocky region of Saurashtra has only two regular mountain ranges, the northern one having about a 357metre peak in the Panchal region. The Bardo with the 625metre Venu peak is about 29km from Porbandar.

The Girnar which is the highest mountain in the state (1,145 metres) forms a part of the range south of the Bardo and is about 160 km in length. The highest peak is named after Guru Dattatreya. Garakhnath, Amba Mata, Kalika Mata, etc. are the names of the other peaks of Girnar. The small hill beside the Girnar, called the Jamial Shah Pir is a Muslim holy place.

The Shetrunjaya hill near Palitana is one of the five sacred hills of Jains. The hills of Talaja, Lor and Sana are known for their Buddhist caves.

Kutch is a saline tract with three mountain ranges. The hills of Kutch are devoid of plant life. Among the three main ranges in Kutch, the northern one goes by Pachham, Khadir and Pranjal. The Kala Parvat forming a part of the ranges lies between Kutch and Sind. The southern range begins at Madh and goes up to Roha.

FOREST

The natural vegetation of the state is restricted to areas which receive adequate rainfall and are at the same time agriculturally unproductive. Ruggedness of terrain and rocky thin soils have made some parts of the state unsuitable for cultivation. Such areas, when occurring in the zone of heavy rainfall support the growth of forests in which the plants like crops do not have to reach maturity and bear fruits in less than a year.

The essential criteria for the growth of forests are suitable conditions of temperature and a heavy rainfall but their distribution is governed by the human selection of cultivated land. In Gujarat, where the rainfall has been essentially guided by orographic features, high rugged areas receive a higher rainfall than the plains. The rainfall in the state increases from the plains to the mountains and from north to south. The forests are therefore concentrated in the hilly parts of the state in the south-east and in the hills of Saurashtra. The hills of Kutch are bare because of low rainfall ascribed to their northern most location and the absence of any orographic features that could come in the way of the monsoon and cause precipitation. South, south-east and east Gujarat are the only areas which have a considerable forest cover.

Gujarat has about 19.66 lakh hectares of land under forest. A large part of the forest cover which is economically exploitable is distributed in the districts of Dangs, Panchmahals, Broach, Surat, Bulsar, Junagadh, Sabarkantha and Banaskantha. Dangs, Surat and Broach, which are the three southern districts of the state have a sizable area under forest.

The districts of Panchmahals and Sabarkantha in north-east Gujarat and Junagadh in Saurashtra are other important areas of forest cover. The south and south-eastern parts of the state support the growth of a tropical deciduous forest typified by teak, shorea robusta for which the district of Bulsar is well known. The forest of the state can be divided into the following broad categories, depending upon their environmental adjustments and the general morphological character of the representative species.

Moist Deciduous Forests: Moist Deciduous Forests occur in Dangs and parts of Vyara in Surat division. These forests are not evergreen and shed their leaves during March and April, through the under-wood and shrub cover are fairly green. Teak is an important species which drops its leaves only in the cold weather in localities which are relatively dry or cold, but is almost evergreen in the moistest parts of its distribution.

Teak needs a moderately good rainfall and a well-drained terrain. The associates of teak in the moist deciduous forests are Terminalia tomestosa and Anogeissus latifolia.

Dry Deciduous Forests: There are a mixed growth of trees which are deciduous during the dry season. The lower canopy in these forests is also deciduous with occasional evergreen or sub greens being present in the moister area. There is an undergrowth of shrubs, but the light reaches the surface allowing the growth of grass which occasionally develops into a savanna-type grass field.

Bamboos are not luxuriant. Other trees of the dry deciduous forests are teak, Boswellia serrata, Anogeissus latifolia and Diospyros malanoxylon. Dry deciduous forests with teak occur in north-east Gujarat, particularly in Sabarkantha district. The forests of Junagadh are valuable for their yield of timber and of grass growing on their outer margin.

Thorny Forests: With the decreasing rainfall in the drier north the forests turn thorny and tend to assume a xerophytic character. Such forests occurring either in Kutch or north Saurashtra and Banaskantha district are characterised by Acacia arabica, Acacia leucophloea, Capparis ophylla, Zizyphus mauratiana etc. The thorny forests of north Gujarat are sparse and provide sites for cattle-grazing. There are bamboo plantations but there are virtually no trees that can yield timber.

The most common variety of Bamboo is Dendorocalamus. The most luxuriant bamboo occur in the interior of the Dangs forests. The density is guided essentially by rainfall. There are larges stands of bamboo in South Gujarat than in the North.

Districts

S.No	District	Area in Sq Km	Population	Headquarter
1.	Ahmedabad	8,707	58,08,378	Ahmedabad
2.	Amreli	6,760	13,93,295	Amreli
3.	Banskantha	12,703	25,02,843	Palanpur
4.	Bharuch	9,038	13,70,104	Bharuch
5.	Narmada	--	5,14,083	Rajpipla
6.	Bhavnagar	11,155	24,69,264	Bhavnagar
7.	Gandhinagar	1,764	13,34,731	Gandhinagar
8.	Jamnagar	14,125	18,16,029	Jamnagar
9.	Junagadh	10,607	24,48,427	Junagarh
10.	Porbandar	--	5,36,854	Porbandar
11.	Kuchchh	45,652	15,26,331	Bhuj
12.	Kheda	7,194	20,23,354	Nadiad
13.	Anand	--	18,56,712	Anand
14.	Mehsana	9,027	18,37,696	Mehsana
15.	Patan	--	11,81,941	Patan
16.	Panchmahal	8,866	20,24,883	Godhara
17.	Dahod	--	16,35,374	Dahod
18.	Rajkot	11,203	25,71,931	Rajkot
19.	Sabarkantha	7,390	20,83,416	Himatnagar
20.	Surat	7,657	49,96,391	Surat
21.	Surendranagar	10,489	15,15,147	Surendranagar
22.	Valsad	5,244	14,10,680	Valsad
23.	Navsari	--	12,29,250	Navsari
24.	Vadodara	7,794	36,39,775	Vadodara
25.	Dang	649	1,86,712	Ahwa

GULF OF KHAMBHAT

The Gulf of Khambhat (formerly known as the Gulf of Cambay) is an inlet of the Arabian Sea along the west coast of India, in the state of Gujarat. It is about 80 miles in length, and divides the Kathiawar peninsula to the west from the eastern part of Gujarat state on the east. The Narmada and Tapti rivers empty into the Gulf. The Gulf is shallow and abounds in shoals and sandbanks. The Gulf is known for its extreme tides, which vary greatly in height and run into it with amazing speed. At low tide the bottom is left nearly dry for some distance below the town of Khambhat.

The Alang Ship Recycling Yard takes advantage of the extreme high tides of the gulf. Large ships are beached during the twice-monthly highest tides, and are dismantled when the tide recedes.

6

Economy

ECONOMY OF GUJARAT

The economy of Gujarat, a state in Western India, has significant agricultural as well as industrial production within India. Major agricultural produce of the state includes cotton, groundnuts (peanuts), dates, sugar cane, milk and milk products. Industrial products include cement and petrol. Gujarat recorded the lowest unemployment rate in India in 2015, with 1.2% of the labour force being unemployed.

Contribution

The world's largest ship breaking yard is in Gujarat near Bhavnagar at Alang.

Reliance Petroleum, one of the group companies of Reliance Industries Limited founded by Dhirubhai Ambanioperates the oil refinery at Jamnagar which is the world's largest grass roots refinery. The company has also planned another SEZ (special economic zone), in Jamnagar.

Gujarat ranks second nationwide in gas-based thermal electricity generation with national market share of over 8% and second nationwide in nuclear electricity generation with national market share of over 1%.

Legatum Institute's Global Prosperity Index 2012 recognised Gujarat as the highest-scoring among all States of India on matters of social capital. The state ranks 15th in a list of 142 nations worldwide and actually ranks higher than several developed nations.

Industrial growth

One of India's most industrialized states, Gujarat maintains a variety of industries, the principal ones being general and electrical engineering and the manufacture of textiles, vegetable oils, chemicals, soda ash, and cement. New industries include the production of fertilizers and petrochemicals. Major resources produced by the state include cotton, peanuts, dates, sugarcane, and petrol. The state is rich in calcite, gypsum, manganese, lignite, bauxite, limestone, agate, feldspar and quartz sand and successful mining of these minerals is done in their specified areas. Gujarat produces about 91% of India's required amount of628+9 soda ash and gives the country about 66% of its national requirement of salt. Chemical Industries in Gujarat count for more than 35% of Indian Chemicals production.

It is one of India's most prosperous states, having a per-capita GDP significantly above India's average. Kalol Khambat and Ankaleshwar are today known for their oil and natural gas production. Dhuvaran has a thermal power station, which uses coal, oil and gas. The Tarapur nuclear station in Maharashtra supplies the remaining power. Also on the Gulf of Khambat, 50 kilometers southeast of Bhavnagar, is the Alang Ship Recycling Yard (the world's largest). General Motors produces the 'Astra' car at Halol near Vadodara. Jalalpur is a large town of Gujarat, where several small and large textile industrial units have been established. Surat, a city by the Gulf of Khambat, is a hub of the global diamond trade.

During the period 1960–90, Gujarat established itself as a leader in various industrial sectors including textiles, engineering, chemicals, petrochemicals, drugs & pharmaceuticals, dairy, cement & ceramics, and gems & jewellery. The post-liberalization period saw Gujarat's state domestic product (SDP) rising at an average growth rate of 14% per annum in real terms (from 1994 to 2002).

Ahmedabad, Ankleshwar and Vapi are the hub of chemical industries in the state, having number of manufacturing units (private as well as state owned) manufacturing dyes, specialty chemicals, agrocutural chemicals, pesticides, pigments, colors, etc. Rajkot city is the hub of engineering manufacturing and has many companies manufacturing auto components, auto engines, CNC machines, forging & casting parts, etc. The state operating companies like GNFC, GSPC, GSFC, GMDC are a few among flagship companies of the state.

Gujarat achieved as much as 35% of augmentation in its power generation capacity during the period 1995–96 and 2000–01. The producers (IPPs) have contributed significantly in this addition. As a matter of fact Gujarat is one of the first few states in India to have encouraged private sector investment and are already in operation. In addition the liquid cargo (chemicals) handling port at Dahej is also set up in joint sector and made operational. At an investor's summit entitled Vibrant Gujaratarranged between January 10, 2007 to January 13, 2007, at Science City, Ahmedabad, the state government signed 104 Memorandum of Understandings for Special Economic Zones totaling worth Rs 2.5 lakh crore. However, most of the investment was from domestic industry.

Agriculture

Gujarat is the main producer of tobacco, cotton, and groundnuts in India. Other major crops produced are rice, wheat, jowar, bajra, maize, tur, and gram. Gujarat has an agricultural economy; the total crop area amounts to more than one-half of the total land area.

Animal husbandry and dairying have played a vital role in the rural economy of Gujarat. Dairy farming, primarily concerned with milk production, functions on a cooperative basis and has more than a million members. Gujarat is the largest processor of milk in India. Amul milk co-operative federation products are well known all over India and is Asia's biggest dairy. Among livestock raised are buffalo and other cattle, sheep, and goats. As per the results of livestock census 1997, there were 209.70

lakh livestock in Gujarat state. As per the estimates of the survey of major livestock products, during the year 2002–03 the Gujarat produced 6.09 million tonnes of milk, 385 million eggs and 2.71 million kg of wool. Gujarat also contributes inputs to industries like textiles, oil and soap.

Automobile

After Tata Motors relocated the Nano manufacturing plant to Sanand, a small town near Ahmedabad, Gujarat has emerged as a car manufacturing hub. Major multinational automobile companies like Suzuki Motor, Ford India, Honda and Hero MotoCorp have plants in operation in Gujarat. Gujarat also leads in upcoming hybrid and electric vehicle manufacturing facilities. Suzuki, in partnership with Denso and Toshiba, is building a lithium ion battery manufacturing facility at a cost of 1700 crore. Suzuki is planning to launch electric cars as well as electric bikes by 2020. The India based JSW Group has signed an agreement to invest Rs 4000 crore to promote manufacturing electric vehicles in the state, which includes vehicle manufacturing, production of batteries, and storage solutions. MG Motors, a subsidiary of China's largest automobile company SAIC Motors, has bought General Motors' manufacturing facility in Halol, Gujarat, and is planning to start production by 2019. Tata Motors is also planning to produce electric cars from its Sanand plant.

Pharmaceutical

Gujarat is ranked number1 in the pharmaceutical industry in India, with a 33% share drug manufacturing and 28% share in drug exports. The state has 117 USFDA certified drug manufacturing facilities.

Tourism

Gujarat is the sixth largest state in India, located in the western part of India, with a coastline of 1600 km (the longest in India). It is one of the most popular states in the country, with an annual footfall of 19.81 million tourists in 2010–11. Gujarat offers scenic beauty from Great Rann of Kutch to the hills of Saputara. It is the world's sole home of pure Asiatic lions.

Gujarat has a large tourist potential.

During the Sultanate reign, Hindu craftsmanship mixed with Islamic architecture, giving rise to the Indo-Saracenic style. Many structures in the state are built in this fashion.

It is also the birthplace of Mahatma Gandhi and Sardar Vallabhbhai Patel, the great iconic figures of India's Independence movement.

Amitabh Bachchan is currently the brand ambassador of Gujarat Tourism. The 'Khushboo Gujarat Ki' campaign by Amitabh Bachchan has grown tourism in Gujarat by 14 per cent, twice the national growth rate.

GUJARAT INFRASTRUCTURE

Gujarat, the westernmost state of India, houses some of the biggest industries of the country. Gujarat infrastructure is quite developed and accommodates a number of industries. The major industrial and infrastructural hubs of the state include Surat, Ahmedabad, Rajkot, Vadodara, Bhavnagar, and Jamnagar.

The state of the art infrastructure projects have helped Gujarat become one of the richest and most developed states in the country. The various industries in the state depend on the infrastructure sectors significantly.

The state's contribution to the country in various industries is as follows:

- 23% of onshore fossil oil production
- 35% of petrochemical production
- 27% of groundnut production
- 41% of chemical goods
- 11% of cotton production
- 15% of freight handling
- 18% of mineral production
- 30% of onshore natural gas
- 26% of pharmaceutical goods
- 25% of cloth production

Petroleum and cement are the major industrial goods of the state. The biggest ship breaking yard is located at Alang near Bhavnagar. The state is affluent in minerals like gypsum, calcite, lignite, manganese, limestone, bauxite, feldspar, agate, and quartz sand.

Major industries of Gujarat

The major industries of the state include the following:

- Engineering
- Cloth making
- Petrochemicals
- Chemicals

- Pharmaceuticals and drugs
- Ceramics and cement
- Dairy
- Ornaments and precious stones

Gujarat Infrastructure Sectors: An Overview

The major infrastructure sectors in the state are as follows:
- Power
- Ports
- Railways
- Roads
- Urban Infrastructure
- Aviation
- Water Supply
- Urban Transportation
- Information Technology Infrastructure
- Industrial Parks

Gujarat is the first state in India which ratified the Gujarat Infrastructure Development Act. The Government did this to support investments in infrastructure projects. In 1995, the Gujarat Infrastructure Development Board (GIDB) was established by way of this act. This organization helps in the influx of funds from the private sector companies to the infrastructure industry and synchronizes the functioning of different agencies.

Education Infrastructure in Gujarat

The literacy rate of Gujarat is 69.1% and it surpasses the countrywide mean of 65.38%. The Indian Institute of Management, Ahmedabad, which is also popularly known as IIM-A, is situated in this state. It is a top business school in the country. Other renowned academic institutions include the following:
- National Institute of Fashion Technology (NIFT)

- National Institute of Design (NID)
- Entrepreneurship Development Institute of India (EDI)

The state of Gujarat houses 26 management schools, 25 engineering colleges, and 300 technical institutes. The state government has chalked out strategies for setting up a shipbuilding university in the Kutch district. They are also planning to establish academic institutes in the following subject areas:

- Port management
- Marine engineering
- Fisheries and fish processing
- Design of precious stones and ornaments
- Disaster management
- Urban planning
- Biotechnology

Healthcare Infrastructure in Gujarat

A number of private public partnership projects are taking place in the healthcare sector in the state. At present, the state is home to 1,072 primary health centres (PHC), 13 medical colleges, 273 community health centres (CHC), 7,274 sub centres, and 85 mobile healthcare divisions. The government has launched the Chiranjeevi Scheme for the purpose of lowering the infant and maternal mortality rate. Private sector and public sector companies will collectively work under this plan and the plan is aimed at financially weaker segments of the society. The table given below will provide a better idea about the success of the Chiranjeevi Scheme:

Area	2005	2007
Infant Mortality Rate (IMR)	64	54 (till the month of August)
Maternal Mortality Rate (MMR)	389	172 (till the month of August)

- Number of deliveries by private specialists - 95,066 (till the month of August 2007)
- Number of private specialists joined - 801 (till the month of August 2007)
- Lives saved by the Chiranjeevi Scheme - 3,443 infants and 548 mothers

Telecommunications Infrastructure in Gujarat

The state has made commendable advancements in the field of telecommunications and some of the highlights of its success are given below:

- Every one of the district headquarters is facilitated with the back-up assistance of mobile V-SAT terminals.
- GSWAN or Gujarat State Wide Area Network is the second biggest IP-oriented WAN in the world, linking more than 2,800 public sector organizations.
- Currently, the redressal of complaints of customers can be performed on the Internet with the SWAGAT (State Wide Grievance Attention on public grievances by application of Technology).
- There are over 7,500 voice connections in the Secretariat Integrated Communication Network (SICN).
- The Integrated Work Flow and Document Management System (IWDMS) have assisted in reshuffling the method of records keeping in the public sector organizations.

Port Infrastructure in Gujarat

The state of Gujarat features an extensive shoreline of 1,600 km and there are 42 ports that are operational and manage more than 80% of port traffic in India.

The small ports in the state manage 20% of the overall freight of the country.

The biggest freight-managing port in the state is the Kandla port. Other than this, the state houses 14 direct berthing captive port terminals, six direct berthing commercial harbors, and 11 lighter age freight ports. It has been projected that by 2015, the ports of the state will manage 39% of the overall freight of the nation.

Tourism Infrastructure in Gujarat

The westernmost state in India can be depicted as a traveler's paradise. The state provides a broad variety of tourism sectors that reflect the culture and tradition of this state. A number of tourism infrastructure projects are underway which include the following:

*   Dholavira – Kutch
*   Mandvi – Kutch
*   Champaner – Panchmahal
*   Somnath and Sasangir – Junagadh
*   Dwarka – Jamnagar

Currently, 24 ecotourism plans are being considered by the government.

Transportation Infrastructure in Gujarat

The state features an extensive roadways network which covers around 74,000 km. The state is well joined with railways as well and houses 5,310 km of rail lines. The roadways network comprises state highways (spanning 18,738 Km), national highways (spanning 2,781 Km), and expressways (covering 93 Km). The goal of the state is to enhance the network and get it to 114,866 Km. Various BOT (Build Own Transfer) and BOOT (Build Own Operate Transfer) projects have been undertaken in the railways and roadways infrastructure sector.

Industrial Infrastructure

Till date, 168 industrial estates have been established by the Gujarat Industrial Development Corporation (GIDC) and another 106 are in pipeline. Special Economic Zones have been established at Surat and Kandla. At present, 55 SEZs are in pipeline. Gandhinagar houses a Software Technology Park.

Bus Rapid Transit System

Ahmedabad Municipal Corporation (AMC), Gujarat Infrastructure Development Board (GIDB,) Ahmedabad Urban Development Authority (AUDA), and the state government are collectively executing the Bus Rapid Transit System (BRTS) in the state.

Power Infrastructure in Gujarat

Power is integral to infrastructure projects and Gujarat's performance of power generation and distribution has been remarkable. According to the statistics of 2007-2008, the state has the capacity of generating 17,403 MW of power, which obviously includes capacity of captive power generation. The state marketed excess power to 12 states and they are the following:

- Tamil Nadu
- Rajasthan
- Maharashtra
- Uttar Pradesh
- Delhi
- Andhra Pradesh
- Karnataka
- Haryana
- Uttarakhand
- Chhattisgarh
- West Bengal
- Madhya Pradesh

The state is the biggest producer of natural gas in the country and Gujarat State Petroleum Corporation (GSPC) has around 42 petroleum and natural gas fields throughout India.

CNG Projects (Urban infrastructure)

Compressed Natural Gas (CNG) has substituted conventional fuel used in auto rickshaws and buses. There are

90 CNG stations in the state and almost 31,513 CNG auto rickshaws and 535 CNG buses are running. In Ahmedabad, it is compulsory to operate just CNG run auto rickshaws.

Water Infrastructure

Water conservation in the state is performed through the following:
- 35,379 bori bandhs (dams constructed by sand bags)
- 87,179 check dams (tiny barrier built over streams with a flow of at least 1 cusec following the rainy season)
- 5,551 dug out ponds.
- 1,30,262 agricultural ponds (khet talavadi)

Private Public Partnerships in Gujarat

A number of private public partnership (PPP) projects have been undertaken in various infrastructure projects in Gujarat and they are as follows:
- Port Sector
- Road Sector
- Power Sector
- Railways Sector
- Road Transport Sector
- IT & ITES Biotech Sector
- Water Sector
- Urban Development Sector
- Aviation Sector
- ULB Urban Development Sector
- Other Infra Project Sector
- Slum rehabilitation

Energy

The basic thing required to run an industry is the energy, because if there is no energy, the machineries will not operate and hence the whole industry will come to stand still. The government of Gujarat has ensured its industries of continuous and cheap supply of electricity for its smooth growth.

Power

Gujarat is one of the largest power generator in India as it has got many natural gas resources beneath its land. Power is generated from these natural gases and then used by different industries as energy. Power is generated at power stations. Power is the force behind the working of every machine. The Gujarat state government have also planned to set up police stations in different zones of Gujarat so as to keep a check on power thefts. The first of its kind police station for power thefts have been set up in Rajkot. Moreover, a 1500 kilometer long gas-grid is being laid to extract more and more natural gas for converting it into power.

Telecommunication

Gujarat has an enviable telecommunications network. Every part of Gujarat state is now connected-either by land line or mobile. The basic telephonic structure of Gujarat state comprises more than 3.5 million landlines, translating into an impressive teledensity of 9 including the services of BSNL and other two private operators namely Tata Teleservices and Reliance Infocomm. Gujarat has abundant energy resources for it is the producer of natural gas and has plans to utilize this gas for power production which in turn would be absorbed as energy by the industries. Underground gas reserves have been found near Ahmedabad and other places. All this is going to produce more energy in Gujarat for public as well as private consumption.

GROWTH AND DEVELOPMENT IN GUJARAT

The reputation of politician Narendra Modi goes beyond the shoreline of India from USA to Sydney, from China suppliers to European countries, one will always find those who are bowled over by Primary Reverend popular Modi's character and style of perform. The success of the Vivid Gujarat Summits shows the worldwide status of politician Narendra Modi; over a hundred nations get involved in the Peak and the results are for all to see. They bring financial commitment and financial development to Gujarat state. Renowned Indian politician Modi similarly turns on the Gujarati local diaspora event due to perform that has occurred in Gujarat. Little wonder that during every amazing Pravasi Indian days, the most expected presenter continues to be great politician Narendra.

He continues to be a commonly journeyed person, having frequented various nations such as Sydney, China suppliers, Asia, country of Mauritius, Thailand country and amazing Uganda. Within a month of supposing office in Oct 2001, Primary Reverend Politician Narendra Modi was an aspect of a delegation to Italy led by the then Primary Reverend politician Atal Bihari Vajpayee where he finalized a milestone pact with the Governor of amazing Astrakan region. The connection between Gujarat state and Italy grew even larger in the following years as Primary Reverend Modi created more formal trips to Italy, even obtaining important co-operation in the area of energy. Renowned Indian politician Modi was among the Native Indian management who frequented Israel as an aspect of an advanced level delegation comprising Native Indian. These days Gujarat is at the limit of creating a powerful collaboration with Israel especially in the areas of hr, farming, water, power and security.

The organization between Southern Eastern Asia and Native Indian go back to hundreds of years and continue to be powerful even now. Primary Reverend renowned politician Modi has frequented Southern Eastern Asia on several activities ever since he took over as CM. He has frequented Hong Kong country, Malaysia country, Singapore country, Taiwan country and Thailand country and these nations have been effective members in various worldwide social activities in Gujarat state such as the yearly International Kite Traveling Event. Chief Reverend Politician Narendra Modi has also started out windows of possibilities for Gujarat state by promoting close financial connections with China suppliers. He has created three formal trips to China suppliers, the last one being in Nov 2011.

During that journey politician, Narendra Modi was accepted by the top authority of China suppliers in the Great Area of the People in China country, an honour usually arranged for Leads of Condition. His China country trips have attracted tremendous financial commitment for Gujarat state along with a renowned MoU with amazing Sichuan region and an important R&D Center with the help of China company renowned Huawei.

With politician Narendra Modi at the helm of matters, state of Gujarat is positioned to lead nationwide renovation. The viewpoint to amazing Change came with the dedication of Politician Narendra Modi who implemented the 'Indian Panchamrut Shakti or also known as power. The five nectars of Gyan power, Jal power, Urja power, Jan power and power of Raksha Shakti or energy for the complete development of situations. State of Gujarat on the European most aspect of Native Indian has one third of shoreline of the nation. Since beginning of situations, the framework of its financial system has modified considerably. Not only the State's GSDP and Per Household GSDP have improved but it has proven all symptoms and symptoms of a designed and urbanized financial system.

PROACTIVE GOVERNANCE

E-governance

Modi believes in using the latest advancements in the technological field for the well being of the masses. Gujarat has the largest optical fibre wide area network in the whole of Asia, stretching over as long as 50,000 km.

This provides him and other Government functionaries a platform to interact not only with the lowest-rung officers of the Government all over the state but also with the people in rural areas through video conferencing. He has introduced a novel concept of SWAGAT.

Gujarat has made e-Governance functional in all its 141 municipalities. The Citizen Facilitation Centres are now functional in all the major centres of Gujarat. At the district level, taluka level and in municipal areas, computerized civic centres have been established where the concept of one-day governance has been implemented. This experiment has been further taken up to the village level by establishing e-grams equipped with Computers and Internet Connectivity.

All 14,000 gram panchayats have been made e-grams. The e-dhara project for total computerization of land records has been extremely successful and widely acclaimed. The other areas of e-Governance include electronic weigh bridges and smart cards for driving licenses, online and roaming ration card system, online filing of sales tax returns, connectivity between courts and jails, creation of huge data base of youths available for employment, online availability of the Government resolutions and forms in digital format, departmental websites disseminating information on various Government schemes and activities etc. A number of awards have been bagged for various e-governance initiatives. The recent ones include the Best e-governed State award from the Government of India in January 2007.

Second Green Revolution

Gujarat is all set to lead the country into the second green revolution. With a holistic approach adopted for water management, the implementation of Jyotigram Yojana (scheme for uninterrupted power supply) for providing round-the-clock 3-phase power and a host of other initiatives including Krishi Mahotsav (agricultural festival), Gujarat has witnessed impressive agricultural performance during the last five years. Agriculture production has increased by 16 lac metric tonnes. GSDP from agriculture at current prices has increased by 128% during the period 2000-01 to 2005-06 reaching a whooping ‘ 33,659 crores. Gujarat is far ahead of the target of 4.03 % average annual growth rate set by the Planning Commission, in the first four years of 10th Five-year Plan. The overall production/cultivation cost has come down dramatically from ‘ 9150 to ‘ 5025 per hectare and the land brought under cultivation has increased significantly.

In order to economize the use of water, Gujarat has also speeded up the promotion, awareness and application of micro-irrigation techniques such as Drip and Sprinkler Irrigation. While the centre has allocated ' 400 crores towards drip irrigation for the entire country, the Government of Gujarat has already started work on drip irrigation schemes worth ' 1500 Crores.

The state government has also created 2.94 lac water harvesting structures like check dams, boribunds and Khet Talavdis (farm ponds) through people's participation. Gujarat now has four Agricultural Universities which are networked for collaborative research. A strategy of "Lab to Land," offering technical assistance to the farmers with the help of scientists of agriculture universities has been introduced. This Lab to Land approach has enabled agri-research from the labs to reach the grass-root levels.

The Government is setting up Agri Export Zones, one covering central and southern Gujarat and two in Saurashtra region are already notified. Yet another initiative unique to Gujarat is the concept of Soil Health Cards. To ensure that the farmers know the quality of their soil and the ideal crop for their soil, a major programme of testing and analysing the health of soil was taken up for all the villages in the state.

Based on the data collected, the government has issued soil health cards to the farmers. These cards contain detailed soil analysis with recommendation for usage of right kind of fertilizers and seeds. More than one lac soil samples have been collected and scientifically analysed and more than 235,000 soil health cards have been distributed. Fruits and spices also saw a major jump in their production as compared to earlier years. Apart from traditional crops, the state is now going to be known for roses, strawberries, organic products and above all bio-diesel.

Development of the Deprived

The man who connotes CM as the common man is not satisfied until the fruits of state's development reach the most

common and those who have been hitherto deprived. There are
different groups of such people and each group requires a special
way to deal with. Going to the root of the problems they face,
his empathetic heart came out with the steps like issue of
roaming ration cards, roaming school cards, insurance cover for
3 lac handicapped, insurance cover for 12.5 million school children,
specital housing colony for the snake charmers, betterment of the
kite preparing community and several other awe-inspiring ideas.

The fact that Gujarat ranks first in the country in the
implementation of 20 point programme for poverty abolition for
the last four years in a row, speaks a lot beyond ranks and
numbers. As per the estimate of the Planning Commission of
India, Gujarat will remain at the top in achieving the targets
of poverty abolition. In fact, the government has already provided
Housing to 46,263 below poverty line families at the cost of '
13672.94 lacs. In the BPL (below poverty line) survey 2002–
07, conducted to identify beneficiaries for rural development
programmes, three new socio-economic parameters were
included in the survey, *viz.*, households headed by widow,
female dependent families and handicapped members. This
door-to-door survey covered 68.65 lac rural households of which
15.93% were identified as extremely poor and 84.07% as poor.
This new BPL list has now been placed online and the selection
of beneficiaries is 'based on this list. This list will be revised
every year and online query of data has been made accessible
to all.

WATER FOR ALL

As a party worker in his early days, Modi had observed that
the shortage of water was the biggest hurdle in the growth and
development of Gujarat. Hence, soon after becoming the Chief
Minister, Modi focused his energies on the problem of water
scarcity that Gujarat was facing. He committed himself to a
mission – 'Water for All' to ensure an enhanced quality of life
for all the citizens of the state; and in just five years, under
his leadership, Gujarat has witnessed a water revolution. He
accelerated the pace of the implementation of Sardar Sarovar

Narmada Project with the dam height today raised to 121.9 metres from 90 metres five years ago, thus making the waters of Narmada river flow all across the state through canals and water transmission lines.

Yet another initiative launched by his Government is the Sujalam Suflam Yojana (literally meaning water for prosperity) which aims to convert the dry and water scarce landscapes of Saurashtra, Kutch and North Gujarat into lush green and flourishing greenscapes. This scheme aims to spread the canal network right from the river Mahi in central Gujarat to the Banas in north Gujarat as well as creating additional storage capacity in various reservoirs and ponds in these areas.

Gujarat was the first state to implement the unique concept of river interlinking. Modi received wide appreciation from one and all when due to his vision, the dried river Saraswati in Northern part of Gujarat, considered very pious, was rejuvenated by bringing the waters of the river Narmada.

He also actively encouraged the application of all kinds of water harvesting, water harnessing and management techniques. Under his visionary leadership, watershed development, construction of check dams, khet talavadis (farm ponds), boribunds (obstructing the flow of water by putting cement filled bags) have become the government's commitment and a people's movement. A statewide drinking water grid is also being established for providing drinking water to more than 14,000 villages and 154 towns. The result is that earlier about 4,000 villages needed to be provided water through tankers which has now reduced to less than 185.

Knowledge Corridors

For higher education, Gujarat has established five more universities. These include Nirma University at Ahmedabad, DDU at Nadiad, DAIICT at Gandhinagar, Shyamji Krishna Verma University at Kutch and Ganpat University at Mehsana. A National Law University has also been established in Gandhi Nagar.

Apart from this, four agricultural universities have also been set up and have formed a network for collaborative research. Several new engineering, pharmacy and technical colleges have been set up and this has led to doubling of the intake capacity in the last five years. An IIT (Indian Institute of Technology) too is being planned in Gujarat. To cater to the demands of a knowledge based economy, new courses have been introduced to develop domain-specific human resources. The stretch between Ahmedabad and Gandhinagar is now being developed as a knowledge corridor. Land has been allotted and several IT parks and centres of excellence are taking shape here. All such measures for human resource development are expected to bring about a revolution in educational standards in Gujarat.

Face Lifting Civic Amenities

Gujarat is not just India's most progressive and industrialized states, it is one of the most urbanized too. The Gujarat Urban Mission aims to provide an enhanced quality of urban life and is essentially a movement that involves people's participation to create clean, green and well managed cities as well as communities that are self sufficient and self reliant. Gujarat is the first state in the country to have made e-Governance functional in all its municipalities and municipal corporations and also the first state to have framed a comprehensive urban health policy.

Financial reforms that have been implemented include accrual based double entry accounting systems and area based property tax calculations. To improve quality of life in urban areas, the year 2005 was declared as the year of Urban Development. This year witnessed conception and rapid implementation of several initiatives; door-to door solid waste collection; creation of Gaurav Paths (roads of pride) and Vikas Paths (roads of development); greening of cities through social a forestation, removal of encroachments; promoting CNG vehicles to reduce pollution; strengthening of water distribution systems; planned housing for the urban poor – all these initiatives are enabling the cities of Gujarat to evolve into global cities. The malls and multiplexes that have come up in recent years have changed the face of the cities of Gujarat.

Apart from this, the Government has set aside a fund of ' 500 crores as the seed money to raise funds from financial institutions as also through public participation to upgrade the urban amenities and services such as cleanliness, sanitation, healthcare, primary education, construction of roads and flyovers, street lights, gardens and parks, sports complexes etc. Ahmedabad is now a mega city and several world-class projects have been put on the fast track including the Sabarmati Riverfront Development and Bus Rapid Transit System. A befitting response to the state initiatives has been given by the corporate world by signing MOUs worth an investment of ' 2.05 lac crores in urban infrastructure projects-ranging from hotels to hospitals. To strengthen the amenities in the entire state and to bring the quality of life in rural areas at par with that in the cities, the year 2007 is being celebrated as "Nirmal Gujarat"–an ongoing initiative for a cleaner and greener Gujarat.

GUJARAT EARTHQUAKE

The biggest challenge which he had to face when he took over as the Chief Minister, was the reconstruction and rehabilitation of the areas affected by the massive Gujarat Earthquake of January 2001.

The Context

On January 26, the Republic day, an extremely severe earthquake struck Gujarat. The earthquake, which measured 6.9 on Richter Scale (India Meteorological Department's estimate) and MW 7.7 (US Geological Survey's estimate), had its epicenter at latitude 23.40N and longitude 70.28E, located to the north of Bhachau, about 250 km west of Ahmedabad, and a depth of 25 km.

The earthquake was followed by more than 500 aftershocks with a magnitude of more than 3.0 and above. The ground shaking lasted about two minutes with strong ground motion lasting for about 25 seconds, and effects from the earthquake were felt throughout the Indian sub-continent. In location and magnitude, this earthquake is very close to the Kutch earthquake on June 19, 1819. This earthquake was the worst natural disaster for the country in the last 50 years. Almost the entire state reeled under its catastrophic impact.

The district of Kutch was devastated. A large number of towns and villages in Kutch suffered almost complete destruction. Other seriously affected districts included Surendranagar, Rajkot, Jamnagar, and Patan. In Ahmedabad, more than 70 high-rise residential buildings collapsed.

The loss of lives caused by the earthquake was colossal. About 13,800 people died1, and approximately 1,67,000 suffered injury. With destruction and damage to more than 1.2 Million houses by the earthquake, the people have lost their shelter and security. All the civic facilities—schools, hospitals, health centres, and public buildings—suffered massive destruction. The utility infrastructure, which included water supply, electricity and telecommunications, were also completely disrupted. The earthquake had a very severe impact on livelihood. More than 10,000 small and medium industrial units stopped production due to damage to plants, factories and machinery. Work at thousands of saltpans stopped after the earthquake. A large number of craftsmen and artisans who live in Kutch lost their workshops and tools. There was a heavy loss of livestock in the region, an important source of peoples' livelihood. In face of these staggering loss estimates, there is a pervasive sense of disempowerment and vulnerability among the people.

The nation rallied to share the grief of the people of Gujarat. As a great expression of human solidarity, relief and support poured in from all over the world. However, as the people recover from the immediate impact of the disaster, the state has to address the issue of long-term rehabilitation. Though the people in the earthquake-affected areas have shown great courage and resilience in dealing with this extreme adversity, they need help and assistance for rebuilding their lives. It has placed an extraordinary responsibility upon the Government of

Gujarat, which responded with a great sense of urgency and sensitivity to the challenge of rehabilitation. With the support of the World Bank, Asian Development Bank, United Nations, and other multilateral and bilateral agencies, it has prepared the Gujarat Earthquake Rehabilitation and Reconstruction Project. It aims at becoming a people's programme. It envisages building of a wide societal coalition for rehabilitation. It emphasizes the empowering process through continuous consultations with the community. It strives for making informed choice for recovery and rehabilitation, through dissemination of technology and best practices. With a deep sense of compassion and commitment, the Government of Gujarat has resolved to lead this programme of rebuilding and regeneration, which will enable people to overcome and transcend this great human tragedy.

Objectives

The Gujarat Earthquake Rehabilitation and Reconstruction Project is a comprehensive multi-sector programme, aimed at rehabilitation of the people affected by the earthquake through provision of housing, social amenities, infrastructure, and livelihood support, based on sustainable economy and ecology.

The program's broad objectives are described as follows:

- Build, retrofit, repair and strengthen houses for the people, and public buildings affected by the earthquake through application of earthquake-resistant technology.

- Revive the local economy by providing assistance for agriculture, industries, small business, and handicrafts, and regenerate livelihood for the people.

- Rebuild and upgrade community and social infrastructure, improve education and health system, and strengthen social protection measures for weaker sections of the population.

- Provide health support to the people injured by the earthquake on a long-term basis and psychological counseling for the people traumatized by the earthquake.

- Restore lifeline infrastructure of transport networks and utility infrastructure of power and water supply, and reduce their vulnerability to natural disasters.
- Support gender empowerment through involving women at all stages in the programme implementation.
- Provide support for the children affected by the earthquake, and alleviate social deprivation through an integrated nutrition and education strategy.
- Implement a comprehensive disaster management programme, improving the disaster preparedness and emergency response capacity of the government to deal with different types of disasters.
- Reduce vulnerability through long-term mitigation programmes aimed at watershed management and drought mitigation, and improve people's resilience and food security through diversification of sources of income-generation and asset building.

Guiding Principles

The mandate of the reconstruction and rehabilitation programme goes beyond the immediate priorities of earthquake reconstruction, and pursues broader social and economic issues impinging on the household-and community-level development and empowerment.

The programme will strive to apply following principles in its implementation:

- It will involve people and representative institutions in the decision-making process, and reflect their priorities and aspirations in programme deliverables.
- It will strengthen civil society institutions like NGOs, community-based organizations, and women's groups through building partnerships and collaborations in the implementation process.
- It will apply principles of equity and empowerment, and ensure, through appropriate mechanisms, that the voices of the weak and poor are always heard.

- It will help the beneficiaries and stakeholders to make informed choices regarding their habitat by disseminating knowledge of seismic technology, building materials and construction practices.
- It will encourage the participation of private sector, NGOs and expert institutions in the programme and expand the ownership and knowledge base of the programme.
- It will introduce structural and non-structural rehabilitation measures, which are feasible and affordable, and which merge with the culture, climate and life-style of communities.
- It will ensure highest levels of transparency and accountability in the programme implementation through appropriate institutional mechanisms and practices.

Programme Components

The Gujarat Earthquake Rehabilitation and Reconstruction Project will comprise a number of components, based on an objective assessment of rehabilitation needs.

These components may be described as follows:

Housing

- Debris removal, salvage and recycling
- Construction of temporary shelters
- Reconstruction of more than 2,30,000 houses
- Repairs and strengthening of over 10,00,000 houses
- Reconstruction and repairs of government staff quarters.

Livelihood Support Programmes

- Credit supply for the self-employed and craftsmen
- Provision of work sheds
- Provision of toolkits for artisans and crafts persons
- Creation of revolving funds for livelihood programmes
- Setting up of handloom-handicraft parks and rural industry centres

- Assistance for farm inputs and implements
- Special package for salt farmers
- Assistance to small, medium and large industries
- Assistance to tourism units
- Assistance to traders and shop owners.

Infrastructure

- Repair and strengthening of roads, bridges and culverts in earthquake-affected areas
- Reconstruction and repair of rural and urban water supply schemes
- Repair and replacement of tube-wells
- Reconstruction and restoration of municipal and environmental infrastructure
- Restoration of transmission and distribution network in power sector
- Reconstruction and strengthening of earthen dams, canals, and irrigation structures
- Repair and Reconstruction of Administrative buildings
- Improved town planning with improved infrastructure in the four towns of Kutch.

Social and Community Development

- Reconstruction of district hospitals, community health centres, primary health centres and primary health sub-centres
- Reconstruction of Aanganwadi Centres, and Integrated Child Development Scheme godowns
- Reconstruction of Ayurvedic and Homeopathic hospitals and dispensaries
- Reconstruction and repair of primary and secondary schools

- Social protection for orphans, widows, handicapped and marginal groups

- Repair and Reconstruction of Higher and Technical Education Institutes with improved infrastructure

- Rehabilitation of protected and private monuments and heritage buildings.

Disaster Management

- Emergency preparedness and response

- Hazard Mapping and Monitoring

- Community-based Disaster Mitigation.

Resource Mobilization

Considering the enormous direct and indirect losses caused by the earthquake, the reconstruction and rehabilitation programme will require a total outlay of about ₹ 8,500/- Crores (US $ 1770 Million).

The Government of Gujarat proposes to secure a loan of about ₹ 3300/- Crores (US $ 687.5 Million) from the World Bank, and ₹ 1680/- Crores (US$ 350 Million) from the Asian Development Bank. Government of India and a number of State Governments too have declared their support and contribution for various components of the rehabilitation programme.

The Government of Gujarat proposes to meet any shortfall in the reconstruction programme through its own resources.

Implementation Strategy

The Government of Gujarat will follow an implementation strategy encompassing all the guiding principles. It is a carefully devised strategy, which harmonizes the emergency nature of reconstruction programme with a strong emphasis on community participation and seismic safety measures.

The main elements of the implementation strategy are as follows:

- Carry out an in-depth damage assessment: The Government has undertaken a comprehensive damage assessment of all the houses, public buildings and infrastructure in the earthquake-affected districts. The damage assessment will provide a more accurate account of the rehabilitation needs, and form the basis of a large-scale engineering and building strategy. It is being carried out by a team for each village, which comprises a Government engineer, an official of Revenue/Panchayat and a representative of NGO/ Headmaster, if no NGO is working within the village.

- Conduct a social impact assessment: The Government has commenced a longitudinal social impact assessment of the earthquake. It will provide a benchmark of vulnerability at the household and community level, and suggest measures, which will help communities to cope with, and recover from the disaster.

- Set up a Public-Private partnership: The Government recognizes the strength of private sector and NGOs in the state in dealing with the enormous challenges of reconstruction. A broad-based partnership with these important institutions of civil society, based on trust and reciprocity, has been an integral feature of the rehabilitation programme.

- Encourage owner-driven and hazard-resistant construction: The Government has actively promoted owner-driven construction, with the application of seismic-resistant technology. It will involve communities in the actual process of construction, and instill a sense of security and confidence among them, which is extremely important for their social and psychological recovery. It will also expand the local knowledge base and capacity for implementing a programme of this magnitude.

- Establish community participation mechanisms and facilitate decision-making at the community level: The Government values the crucial role to be played by formal and informal processes of community participation at the level of villages and urban centres. The Government will strive to encourage these processes, which enable communities to take their decisions regarding reconstruction and development within the broad rehabilitation policy framework and ensure accountability and probity in the implemen-tation.

- Disseminate information about the rehabilitation programme and people's entitlements: The Government has organized an active campaign of information dissemination regarding different packages of assistance and the peoples' entitlement. It recognizes the importance of community outreach for application of hazard resistant technology in construction and active participation of people in the rehabilitation programme. The Government also seeks to involve the elected representatives, media, and academia in the rehabilitation programme through outreach and education programmes.

- Emphasize social and community development and gender empowerment: The Government has integrated a strong component of social and community development in the rehabilitation programme. It places the reconstruction programme right in the context of development and empowerment. It also recognizes the importance of women's participation in the programme as a crucial indicator of the peoples' ownership of the programme.

- Constitute the Gujarat State Disaster Management Authority (GSDMA): The Government has set up an empowered organization, GSDMA, under the chairmanship of Chief Minister, especially for implementing the massive earthquake rehabilitation programme. The GSDMA draws upon a diverse pool of experience and specialization from the government and private sector, and encourages flexibility, innovation and responsiveness in its operations, while maintaining the highest level of professional standard. Supported by a number of project consultants, it coordinates among all the implementing agencies, and provides leadership of the project.

TRANSPORT

Air

Sardar Vallabhbhai Patel International Airport, Ahmedabad

Gujarat has seventeen airports. The Gujarat Civil Aviation Board (GUJCAB) has been formed to foster development of aviation infrastructure in Gujarat. The Board is headed by the Chief Minister.

International airports

- Sardar Vallabhbhai Patel International Airport at Ahmedabad
- Surat Domestic Airport at Surat

Domestic airports operated by the Airports Authority of India (AAI)

- Bhavnagar Airport — 9 km from the city of Bhavnagar

- Bhuj Airport — Located on Airport Ring Road Bhuj city
- Deesa Airport – 5 km from Deesa
- Harni Airport – Integrated Terminal Airport (Vadodara)
- Jamnagar Airport – About 8 kilometres from the Jamnagar city
- Kandla Airport (Gandhidham) — Situated at Kandla, near Gandhidham, in Kutch district
- Keshod Airport (Junagadh) — Keshod Airport is found 3 km from Keshod city in Junagadh District
- Porbandar Airport — Situated 5 km from the city of Porbandar
- Rajkot Airport — 4 km from the city of Rajkot
- Vadodara Airport at Vadodara

State-operated airports

- Mehsana Airport — Mehsana Airport is about 2 km from Mehsana city
- Mandvi airport

Rail

Gujarat comes under the Western Railway Zone of the Indian Railways. Vadodara Railway Station is the busiest railway station in Gujarat and the fourth busiest railway station in India. It is situated on the Mumbai – Delhi Western Railway Mainline. Other important railway stations are Surat railway station, Ahmedabad Railway Station and Rajkot Railway Station. Indian Railways is planning Delhi–Mumbai dedicated rail freight route passing through the state.

The 39.259 km (24.394 mi) long tracks of the first phase of MEGA, a metro rail system for Ahmedabad and Gandhinagar is under construction. It is expected to complete by December 2018. The construction started on 14 March 2015.

Sea

Kandla Port

Gujarat State has the longest sea coast of 1600 km in India. Kandla Port is one of the largest ports serving Western India. Other important ports in Gujarat are the Port of Navlakhi, Port of Magdalla, Port Pipavav, Bedi Port, Port of Porbandar, Port of Veraval and the privately owned Mundra Port. The state also has Ro-Ro ferry service.

Road

Gujarat State Road Transport Corporation (GSRTC) is the primary body responsible for providing the bus services within the state of Gujarat and also with the neighbouring states. It is a public transport corporation providing bus services and public transit within Gujarat and to the other states in India. Apart from this, there are a number of services provided by GSRTC.

- Mofussil Services — It connects major cities, smaller towns and villages within Gujarat.
- Intercity Bus Services — It also connects major cities —

Ahmedabad, Surat, Veraval, Vapi, Vadodara (Baroda) and Rajkot.

- Interstate Bus Services — It connects various cities of Gujarat with the neighbouring states of Madhya Pradesh, Maharashtra and Rajasthan.
- City Services — GSRTC also provides city bus services at Surat, Vadodara, Vapi, Gandhinagar and Ahmedabad, within the state of Gujarat.
- Parcel Services — This service is used for transporting goods.

Apart from this, the GSRTC provides special bus services for festivals, industrial zones, schools, colleges and pilgrim places also buses are given on contract basis to the public for certain special occasions.

- There are also city buses in cities like Ahmedabad (AMTS and Ahmedabad BRTS), Surat (Surat BRTS), Bhavnagar (VTCOS) Vadodara (Vinayak Logistics), Gandhinagar (VTCOS), Rajkot (RMTS and Rajkot BRTS), Anand (VTCOS) etc.

Auto rickshaws are common mode of transport in Gujarat. The Government of Gujarat is promoting bicycles to reduce pollution by the way of initiative taken by free cycle rides for commuters..

7

Tourism

INTRODUCTION

Gujarat is one of the most popular states in India for tourism with an annual footfall of 19.81 million tourists in 2010–11. It offers scenic beauty from the Great Rann of Kutch to the hills of Saputara and is the sole home of pure Asiatic lions in the world. During the historic reigns of the sultans, Hindu craftsmanship blended with Islamic architecture, giving rise to the Indo-Saracenic style. Many structures in the state are built in this fashion. It is also the birthplace of Mahatma Gandhi and Sardar Vallabhbhai Patel, great iconic figures of India's Independence movement. Amitabh Bachchan is currently the brand ambassador of Gujarat Tourism. The 'Khushboo Gujarat Ki' campaign by Bollywood megastar Amitabh Bachchan has enhanced tourism in Gujarat by 14 per cent, twice that of national growth rate.

Museums

Gujarat has a variety of museums on different genres that are run by the state's Department of Museums located at the principal state museum, Baroda Museum & Picture Gallery in Vadodara, which is also the location of the Maharaja Fateh Singh Museum. The Kirti Mandir, Porbandar, Sabarmati Ashram, and Kaba Gandhi No Delo are museums related to Mahatma Gandhi, the former being the place of his birth and the latter two where he lived in his lifetime. Kaba Gandhi No Delo in Rajkot exhibits part of a rare collection of photographs relating to the life of Mahatma Gandhi. Sabarmati Ashram is the place where Gandhi initiated the Dandi March. On 12 March 1930 he vowed that he would not return to the Ashram until India won independence.

Statue of Mahatma Gandhi in Sabarmati Ashram

Lakhota Museum in Jamnagar

The Maharaja Fateh Singh Museum is housed within Lakshmi Vilas Palace, the residence of the erswhile Maharajas, located in Vadodara.

The Calico Museum of Textiles is managed by the *Sarabhai Foundation* and is one of the most popular tourist spots in Ahmedabad.

The Lakhota Museum at Jamnagar is a palace transformed into museum, which was residence of the Jadeja Rajputs. The collection of the museum includes artefacts spanning from 9th to 18th centuries, pottery from medieval villages nearby and the skeleton of a whale.

Other well known museums in the state include the Kutch Museum in Bhuj, which is the oldest museum in Gujarat founded in 1877, the Watson Museum of human history and culture in Rajkot, Gujarat Science City and Sardar Vallabhbhai Patel National Memorial in Ahmedabad.

Religious sites

Dwarkadhish Temple

Religious sites play a major part in the tourism of Gujarat. Somnath is the first amongst twelve Jyotirlingas, and is mentioned in the Rigveda. The Palitana temples of Jainism on Mount Shatrunjaya, Palitana are considered the holiest of all pilgrimage places by the Svetambara and Digambara Jain community. Palitana is the world's only mountain with more than 900 temples. The Sidi Saiyyed Mosque and Jama Masjid are holy mosques for Gujarati Muslims. The Sun Temple, Modhera is a ticketed monument, handled by the Archaeological Survey of India. Dwarakadheesh Temple and Dakor holy pilgrimage sites are for devotees of Lord Krishna. Other religious sites in state include Mahudi, Shankheshwar, Ambaji, Dakor, Shamlaji, Chotila etc.

DEVELOPMENT OF TOURISM IN GUJARAT

Majestic Laxmi Vilas Palace(Built By Maharaja Sayajirao Gaekwad III), Baroda

Mahatma Gandhi's Visitor Room at Hridaya Kunj

Gujarat is the 6th largest state in India, located in the western part of India with a coastline of 1600 km (longest in India). It is one of the most popular tourist regions in the country and was visited by 20 million domestic and international tourists in 2010-11. Gujarat offers scenic beauty from Great Rann of Kutch to the hills of Saputara. Gujarat is the one and only place to view pure Asiatic lions in the world. During the Sultanate reign, Hindu craftsmanship mixed with Islamic architecture, giving rise to the Indo-Saracenic style. Many structures in the state are built in this fashion. It is also the birthplace of Mahatma Gandhi and Sardar Vallabhbhai Patel, iconic figures of India's independence movement.

Amitabh Bachchan is currently the brand ambassador of Gujarat Tourism. The 'Khushboo Gujarat Ki' campaign by celebrity Amitabh Bachchan has increased tourism in Gujarat by 14 per cent per annum, twice that of national growth rate.

Ahmedabad with its central location and a well connected international airport is considered to be an ideal hub to cover all the destinations in Gujarat.

Business tourism

Gujarat is one of the most industrialized states in the country. There are many Indian and global companies located in Gujarat and the area has seen double digit GDP growth in past decade. It is also known as "Growth Engine of India".

Vibrant Gujarat is biennial investors' summit held by the government of Gujarat. The event is aimed at bringing together business leaders, investors, corporations, thought leaders, policy and opinion makers; the summit is advertised as a platform to understand and explore business opportunities in the state. It has become a model for economic success for many states. According to the list of the top 10 Indian cities by GDP in 2009, based on a PricewaterhouseCoopers study, Ahmedabadranks 7th in India with an annual GDP of 59 billion USD.

Gujarat International Finance Tec-City is an under-construction city in Gujarat. It will be located next to the Sabarmati river, 12 km north of Ahmedabad and 8 km South of Gandhinagar, the political capital of the state. It will be built on 500 acres (2.0 km) of land. Its main purpose is to provide high-quality physical infrastructure so that finance and tech firms can relocate their operations there from Mumbai, Bangalore, Gurgaon and other regions where infrastructure is either inconsistent or very expensive.

Hill stations

The Palitana temple complex
- Wilson Hills
- Saputara
- Pavagadh
- Palitana

Archeological and heritage tourism

Within Gujarat there are a wide variety of historic forts, palaces, mosques, temples, and places of historical importance in India's struggle for independence. Many of these palaces and forts have been converted into heritage hotels to keep tourists close to the vibrant history of Gujarat. For example, Laxmi Vilas Palace, Vadodara is reputed to have been the largest private dwelling built at the time and it is four times the size of Buckingham Palace in London. These sites are under-developed and are considered to have huge development potential. World heritage sites like Lothal, Dholavira and Champaner are also located within Gujarat.

Cultural tourism

Ajrak

Gujarat is well known for its rich culture. The folk arts of Gujarat form a major part of the culture of the state. It preserves the rich tradition of song, dance, drama as well. Handicrafts include Bandhani, patolas of Patan, kutchhi work, Khadi, bamboo craft, block printing, embroidery, woodcraft, metal crafts, pottery, namda, rogan painting, pithora and many more handicrafts. The Arabs, Portuguese, Dutch, Mughals and British as well as Parsis have left their mark on Gujarat's culture.

Religious tourism

Shrimad Rajchandra Jain Spiritual Ashram, one of the largest spiritual and meditation centres in Gujarat at Dharampur.

Gujarat - Home to multitude devotional centres and temples with famous religious centers like Dwarka, Dakor, Ambaji, Palitana, Mahudi, Shankheshwar, Hutheesing Jain Temple, Somnath, Girnar, Shamlaji, Bahucharaji, Pavagadh, Kabirvad, Sun Temple, Modhera, Akshardham (Gandhinagar), Shri

Swaminarayan Mandir, Ahmedabad, Vasai Jain Temple, Jain temples, Hindu Temples and Sudama Mandir. Ashapura mataji madh- Kutch, Swaminarayan Mandir - Bhuj, Narayan Sarovar, Tulsi Shyam, Sattadhar, Lojpur, Junagadh Buddhist Cave Groups etc.

Somnath

The Palitana temples of Jainism on Mount Shatrunjaya, Palitana are considered the holiest of all pilgrimage places by the Svetambara Jain community. Palitana is the world's only mountain with more than 900 temples.

Gujarat is also known for world-famous shrine of shehenshah e Gujarat hazrat syed Ali meera datar and it comes under government heritage site.Shrine of hazrat syed ali meera datar baba is one the few shrines in India where thousands of people from all religions visit daily to take blessings.Followers of shrine believe that each and every problem and suffering of human life can be solved by spiritual force of shrine.Shrine is situated in a small village named unavailable(mehsana) which is about 90 km from Ahmedabad.

Wildlife tourism

Gujarat is habitat for the world's rarest as well large number of fauna and flora. Fauna includes Asiatic lions, wild ass, blackbuck, bears, monkeys, nilgai, paradise flycatcher, chinkara, dolphins, whale shark and migratory birds like flamingos, pelican, and storks. Flora includes species of khair, sadad, timru, babul, salai, khakro, ber, asundro and bordi. The state also has national park. Sanctuaries at Gir National Park, Marine National Park, Gulf of Kutch, Vansda National Park, Nalsarovar Bird Sanctuary, Kutch Bustard Sanctuary, Purna Wildlife Sanctuary and Blackbuck National Park, Velavadar.

Flamingoes

Tourism Department along with Forest Department of Gujarat are maintaining many campsites to promote ecotourism in Gujarat.

Fairs and festivals

Garba (dance)

Gujarat celebrates unique festivals like "Navratri Garba"

(October–November,all over the state),"Diwali" (November), "Kite Festival (Makar Sankranti,11–15 January, Ahmedabad), "Kankaria Carnival" (25–31 December, Ahmedabad), "Rann Utsav" (November–December, Kutch), "Modhera Dance Festival" (3rd week January, Modhera) and fairs like Tarnetar Fair (August, Tarnetar) & Vautha Mela (November, Vautha).

Medical tourism

Ahmedabad leading city of the state is the most preferred place for medical tour or medical treatments in India. With world class health facilities and affordable cost, the city is becoming one of the most sought medical tourism center in the country. The 108 Service is the highly appreciated 'Medical at doorstep' Service. More than 1500 foreigners visit the state per year for various treatments in the state. Ahmedabad Civil Hospital is the biggest hospital in Asia located at Ahmedabad. There are many new upcoming hospitals coming in the city too.

Royal Orient Train

The Royal Orient Train is an Indian luxury tourism train that runs between Gujarat and Rajasthan, covering important tourist locations in the two states. The train started in 1994-95 as a joint venture of the Tourism Corporation of Gujarat and the Indian Railways. There are 13 coaches in the train, named after erstwhile kingdoms of Rajputana. The coaches provide five-star hotel comforts to passengers. Cabins are furnished in a palatial style and have spacious baths attached. There are multi-cuisine restaurants that offer Rajasthani, Gujarati, Indian, Chinese and continental cuisine. The Royal Orient train also has a bar on board, as well as a lounge in every coach where passengers can read books and magazines, watch television, listen to music and interact with other passengers. Other facilities include an intercom, channel music, TV, DVD system and a massage-cum-beauty parlor. The Royal Orient offers a 7-day/8-night package that covers important heritage tourist locations in Rajasthan and Gujarat. The train starts from Delhi Cantonment station and has stops at Chittorgarh, Jaipur, Udaipur,

Ahmedabad, Mehsana, Junagarh, Veraval, Sasan Gir, Mandvi, Palitana and Sarkhej.

STATUE OF UNITY

The Statue of Unity is a statue of Indian statesman and founding father Sardar Vallabhbhai Patel (1875–1950) in the Narmada district of Gujarat, India. It is the world's tallest statue, with a height of 182 metres (597 ft) or about two times as tall as the Statue of Liberty (including the pedestal). The statue is on a river island facing the Narmada Dam (also called the Sardar Sarovar dam) near Rajpipla, 100 kilometres (62 mi) southeast of the city of Vadodara.

The monument and its surroundings occupy more than 2 hectares (4.9 acres), and are surrounded by a 12 km(4.6 sq mi; 3,000 acres) artificial lake. It was built by Larsen & Toubro, who received the contract for 2,989 crore(US$420 million) for the design, construction and maintenance in October 2014. The construction was started on 31 October 2014 and completed in mid-October 2018. It was designed by Indian sculptor Ram V. Sutar, and was dedicated by Indian Prime Minister Narendra Modi on 31 October 2018, the 143rd anniversary of Patel's birth.

Origin and outreach

The project was first announced on 7 October 2010. The Sardar Vallabhbhai Patel Rashtriya Ekta Trust (SVPRET) was established by the Gujarat government for construction of the statue. A drive named the Statue of Unity Movement was started to support the construction of the statue. It helped collect the iron needed for the statue by asking Indian farmers to donate their used farming instruments. Ultimately 5,000 tonnes (4,900 long tons; 5,500 short tons) of iron were collected. Although it was initially intended for the statue, it was later decided that the collected iron would instead be used for other parts of the project.

Fig. Aerial view of the Statue of Unity, 2018.

Fig. Run for Unity in December 2013

The Statue of Unity Movement organised a *Suraaj* ("good governance" in Hindi) petition which was signed by an estimated 20 million people, which was the world's largest petition. A marathon entitled *Run For Unity* was held on 15 December 2013 in several places throughout India.

Design and construction

The statue depicts Vallabhbhai Patel, one of the most prominent leaders of the Indian independence movement, the first Deputy Prime Minister of India, and responsible for the unification of hundreds of princely states to form the modern political boundary of India.

Fig. Vallabhbhai Patel was one of the founding fathers of the Republic of India

Design

The total height of the structure from its base is 240 m (790 ft), with a base of 58 m (190 ft) and statue of 182 m (597 ft). It was designed by Indian sculptor Ram V. Sutar.

Fundraising

The statue was built on a Public Private Partnership model, with most of the money raised by the Government of Gujarat. The Government of India had allotted 3 billion (US$42 million) for the project in the budget from 2012 to 2016. In the 2014–15 Union Budget, 2 billion (US$28 million) were allocated for the construction of the statue.

STATUE OF UNITY, THE WORLD'S LARGEST, UNVEILS IN INDIA AS A FITTING TRIBUTE TO SARDAR PATEL ON HIS BIRTH ANNIVERSARY

Prime Minister Narendra Modi, today, dedicated to the nation a 182-metrestatue of Sardar Vallabhbhai Patel, believed to be the tallest in the worldand said it will be a reminder about the courage of a man who thwarted efforts to disintegrate India.

In his speech, Modi stressed that the statue would generate immense employment opportunities for the local tribals living near the dam in Narmada district. Gujarat's governor OP Kohli, chief minister Vijay Rupani and BJP chief Amit Shah were also present at the unveiling of the Statue of Unity.

Fig. PM Modi, today, dedicated to the nation a 182-metre statue of Sardar Vallabhbhai Patel, the tallest in the world and said it will be a reminder about the courage of a man who thwarted efforts to disintegrate India.

PM Modi described the Statue of Unity as a symbol of the country's engineering and technical capabilities.

To welcome visitors, the Gujarat government has not only built a 3-star hotel, shopping centre and a research centre in the Sardar Patel statue complex, but has also built high-speed elevators that will take you to a height of about 400 feet through the core of the statue where you can get a panoramic view of the surroundings.

What is unique about the statue?

Apart from being the world's tallest statue, it also holds the distinction of being among the fastest to be completed -just 34 months unlike China's Spring Temple Buddha which took 11 years. The work began on December 19, 2015.

Where is the statue built?

The imposing monument is twice the height of the Statue of Liberty in the US and is built on an islet, Sadhu Bet, around 3.5 km downstream from the Sardar Sarovar Dam in Gujarat's Narmada district. The best way to reach Sadhu Bet island is to take a boat ride. Built at a cost of Rs. 2,989 crore, the statue depicts Sardar Vallabhbhai Patel, India's first home minister, wearing a traditional dhoti and shawl, towering over the Narmada River.

One of the greatest living Indian sculptors, Shri Ram Vanji Sutar created over 50 sculptures.

His works include restoring sculptures found in Ellora & Ajanta, Chambal monument at the Gandhi Sagar Dam, busts of Bapu and Gurudev Tagore and 'Statue of Unity.' Congratulations to him! Padma Bhushan awardee, Ram Vanji Sutar, a 93-year-old acclaimed sculptor who graduated from the prestigious J.J School of Art in Bombay designed the statue. He has sculpted masterpieces including that of Mother Chambal at Gandhi Sagar Dam in Madhya Pradesh, equestrian statue of Maharaja Ranjit Singh in Amritsar, and numerous statues of Mahatma Gandhi.

Who built the statue?

It has been built by Larsen and Toubro and the state-run Sardar Sarovar Narmada Nigam Ltd. It took about 250 engineers and 3,400 labourers to construct the statue.

Malaysia-based Eversendai, which constructed Dubai's famous Burj Al Arab and Burj Khalifa buildings, was handed the contract for the steel framework.

Fig. It took about 250 engineers and 3,400 labourers to construct the Statue of Unity.

Construction materials used to build the statue

It has been built using over 70,000 tonnes of cement, 18,500 tonnes of reinforcement steel, 6,000 tonnes of structural steel and 1,700 metric tonnes of bronze, which was used for the outer cladding of the structure.

The Sardar Vallabhbhai Patel Rashtriya Ekta Trust (SVPRET), set up by Modi in 2011 arranged some 129 tonnes of iron implements from nearly 100 million farmers in 169,000 villages across all states to construct the base of the statue.

How was the design finalised?

The statue is conceived as a naturalistic depiction of Sardar Patel in a walking pose. To get it right, designers sifted through 2,000 photographs of Sardar Patel before picking the one that they would model it on and then converted the two-dimensional photograph into a three-dimensional model.

What will be its cost of operation and maintenance?

Rs 657 crore over 15 years, Rs 43.8 crore annually or Rs 12 lakh per day.

Costing of tickets

- The statue will be open for the public visit from November 3. People will have to book tickets online to visit the statue - at www.soutickets.in
- Entry ticket for adults is priced at Rs 120 while for children (between three to 15 years), it is Rs 60
- The ticket includes entry to the 'Valley of Flower', memorial, museum and an audio-visual gallery, SOU site and the Sardar Sarovar Dam
- For observation deck view, the ticket is priced at Rs 350
- Tickets to avail the bus services cost Rs 30 for adults and Re 1 for children
- If you have booked an entry ticket or observation deck ticket, then the bus ticket need not be booked separately

Timings to visit the statue

The Statue of Unity can be visited from 9 am to 6 pm on all days.

Selfie point for pictures

For those who want to click photographs, the complex also has a separate selfie point from where you get a good view of the statue and its surroundings.

8

Population and Religion

POPULATION OF GUJARAT 2018

Gujarat is a state located in West India, also known as the Jewel of Western India. Gujarat has a zone of 196,024 km 2 with a coastline of 1,600 km, most of which lies on the Kathiawar promontory and a population of 60 million. The state is flanked by Rajasthan, Maharashtra, Madhya Pradesh toward the east and the Pakistani area of Sindh toward the west. Its capital is Gandhinagar and the biggest city is Ahmedabad. It includes some of the places of the old Indus Valley Civilization, for instance, Lothal and Dholavira.

Gujarat is also known for its scenic views and spectacular attractions, especially in the rural parts of Gujarat.

Population Of Gujarat In 2018

The number of inhabitants in Gujarat State was 60,383,628, as per the 2011 evaluation information. According to the registration of 2011, the state has a sex proportion of 918 females for 1000 males, one of the least (positioned 24) among the 29 states in India.

Talking about population, in order to check out the population of Gujarat in 2018, we need to have a look at the population of the past 5 years. They are as per the following:

1. 2013 – 62.7 Million
2. 2014 – 63.9 Million
3. 2015 – 65.2 Million
4. 2016 – 66.1 Million
5. 2017 – 67.16 Million

Predicting the 2018 population of Gujarat is not easy but we can get the idea after analysing the population from the year 2013 – 17. As we have seen that every year the population increases by approximate 0.892 Million people. Hence, the population of Gujarat in 2018 is forecast to be 67.16 Million + 0.892 Million = 68.052 Million. So, the population of Gujarat in the year 2018 as per estimated data is 68.052 Million.

Demography Of Gujarat

While Gujarati speakers constitute a bigger piece of the state's population, the metropolitan zones of Ahmedabad and Surat are cosmopolitan, with different other ethnic and vernacular gatherings. Marwaris make broad minorities out of monetary vagrants, littler gatherings of Nepalese, Portuguese, South Koreans, Assamese, Armenians, Greeks, Tibetans and Parsis furthermore live here. The South Korean community usually worked in the tanning business and ran restaurants.

Population Density And Growth Of Gujarat

The population density of the state is 258 persons per square kilometre. Gujarat is the tenth greatest state with respect to Population in India. It is a standout among the most industrialised states and in this way attracts individuals from India both with respect to ventures and vocations. From a little figure of 50,671,017 in 2001, the number of people in the state has touched 60,383,628 in 2011. Population growth in Gujarat has seen an extension of 19.17 in this decade. The population is developing at a yearly rate of 1.9 percent. In 2016, Going by its yearly development rate, it would touch 70 Million. This is an incredible figure.

Facts About Gujarat:

1. 80% of every single valuable stone sold anyplace on the planet are cleaned in Gujarat. The solitary non-Jews in the Tel Aviv and Jerusalem valuable stone are from Gujarat.

2. At the stature of around 2000 feet, Palitana in Gujarat is the fundamental spot on the planet with more than 900 Jain temples.

3. Gandhinagar is considered as one of the greenest cities on the planet and the greenest capital city in Asia.

4. India and Pakistan's Father of Nations both were Gujarati, specifically, Mohandas Karamchand Gandhi also called Mahatma Gandhi and Muhammad Ali Jinnah.

5. The rate of man-days lost in the state as a result of work fomentation/strike is 0.42%, the most lessened in the country.

DEMOGRAPHICS

The population of Gujarat was 60,383,628, according to the 2011 census data. The population density is 308 km (797.6/sq mi), lower than other Indian states. As per the census of 2011, the state has a sex ratio of 918 girls for every 1000 boys, one of the lowest (ranked 24) amongst the 29 states in India.

While Gujarati speakers constitute a majority of Gujarat's population, the metropolitan areas of Ahmedabad and Surat are cosmopolitan, with numerous other ethnic and language groups. Marwaris compose large minorities of economic migrants; smaller communities of people from the other states of India has also migrated to Gujarat for employment. Portuguese, Anglo-Indians, Jews and Parsis also live in the areas. Sindhi presence is traditionally important here following the Partition of India in 1947.

RELIGION

Religion in Gujarat (2011)

Hinduism (88.57%)

Islam (9.67%)

Jainism (0.96%)

Christianity (0.52%)

Sikhism (0.10%)

Buddhism (0.05%)

Others (0.03%)

Not stated (0.10%)

Palitana Temples

According to 2011 census, the religious makeup in Gujarat was 88.6% Hindu, 9.7% Muslim, 1.0% Jain, 0.5% Christian, 0.1% Sikh, 0.05% Buddhist and 0.03% others. Around 0.1% did not state any religion. Hinduism is the major religion of the state, as about 89% population of the state is Hindu. A major part of the Hindu population follow Vaishnavism. Muslims are the biggest minority in the state accounting for 9.5% of the population. Gujarat has the third-largest population of Jains in India, following Maharashtra and Rajasthan.

The Zoroastrians, also known in India as Parsi and Irani, are believed to have migrated to Gujarat to escape adverse conditions in Persia and maintain their traditions. They have also played an instrumental role in economic development, with several of the best-known business conglomerates of India run by Parsi-Zoroastrians, including the Tata, Godrej, and Wadia families. There is a small Jewish community centred around Magen Abraham Synagogue.

Hathisingh Jain Temple, Ahmedabad

Gurudwara Govinddham, Ahmedabad

GUJARAT RELIGIONS

Like all other states of India, Gujarat is also inhabited by people of different religions, castes and creeds. It is one of the most industrialized states of India and provides employment opportunities for the youth. As a result, people from across the country have settled in the state. People in Gujarat mainly follow Hinduism and about 89.1% of the population is formed by the Hindus. They are mostly conservative and strictly adhere to vegetarian diet. The main deity of the Hindus of Gujarat is Lord Krishna. He is worshipped throughout the state, in the form of Shrinathji. Besides Hindus, Gujarat is also home to a considerable number of Muslims and Jains. Muslims constitute about 9.1% of the population, while Jains form nearly 1.0%. Sikhs are quite small in number and just constitute 0.1% of the population. This confirms the reason for cultural diversity of Gujarat.

Gujarat is the birthplace of Gandhiji and the Swaminarayan sect of Hinduism. This has significantly contributed to the fact that Hinduism is widely followed in the state. Lord Krishna also built his terrestrial kingdom here, which has contributed significantly to the religious beliefs of the people. As major trade practices were carried out in Gujarat during the ancient times, a significant number of Parsi Zoroastrians are found in Gujarat.

The people of Gujarat are divided into three major groups in terms of religion - the Hindus, Jains and the Muslims, with the size of the communities divided in that order.

Hinduism

The major population of Gujarat comprises of Hindus. From earlier times, 'Vedic Dharma' was popular and from the remains found from the Indus Valley Civilization, it is believed that worship of goddesses, Sun and Shiva was followed. The temple of Somnath, one of the twelve 'jyotirlingas' of Shiva; the eleventh-century Sun-Temple, at Modhera; and the oldest temple of Dwarkadhish are some of the places sacred to the Hindus.

Jainism

Jainism is widely followed in Gujarat for years. The oldest temple is believed to be of Shankheshwar Parshvanath in North Gujarat. Taranga temples were built during the Solanki period and they are better preserved than the temples of Mount Abu, Girnar and Shatrunjay. Palitana, is India's principal Jain pilgrimage site housing temples antedating 5th century.

Islam

Through the sea-route, which was open for trade, the people from Iran and Arabic countries started coming to Gujarat. The trade system was established and the Indo-Islamic culture flourished. The famous mosques are built during Mughal times. These include Sidi Sayyid's mosque, Jami Masjid, of Ahmedabad , Alif Khan's Mosque in Dholka, Jama Masjid of Bharuch, etc.

Buddhism

Buddhism also became popular about the same time as Jainism. There were Buddhist temples also and the remains of the same are found all over Gujarat. Ashokan Buddhist edicts engraved on a rock, dating back to 3rd century BC, are near Junagadh.

9

Art, Architecture, Fair and Festivals

GUJARAT ARTS AND CRAFTS

One of the oldest states in India Gujarat represents Indian culture at its best. Gujarat is blessed with a rich cultural and traditional past. The state boasts of an age old glorious cultural that has managed to survive till date. The art and crafts of Gujarat are unique to the state and are popular not only within the Indian subcontinent but all across the globe. Most of the artisans in the state are usually villagers who initially created these masterpieces of art and craft for their households which later on only turned out to become a major industry of the state. The art and crafts industry of Gujarat offers a number of jewelry, metalwork, embroidery, furniture, clay items, handmade durries (carpets), stone crafts and other materials. The brass industry of Jamnagar is one of the largest in India.

Brass and Iron Items

Gujarat is one of the major producers of Brass and Iron items in the country. Mostly produced in the princely state of Saurashtra and Kutch brass and iron the most common items available here are copper coated iron bells, beetle nut crackers and cutlery knives. These magnificent works of art are created by the descendents of the erstwhile court jewelers and sword smiths. The place is also popular for its range of Brass items which include brass and iron utensils, cutlery, knives and scissors.

Clay Items

The art of Pottery is among the oldest and most appreciated art and crafts of Gujarat. The artisans who are generally ordinary rural locals are masters of the art of molding clay into well proportioned utensils. After the creation of these utensils they are painted with vibrant colors that add to the beauty of the pot. The artisist of Kutch are renowned worldwide not only for their pottery but also for their variety of Terracotta toys.

Embroidery

Embroidery and textiles is one of the most booming industries of Gujarat. Embroidery in Gujarat in is mostly practiced by women who live in villages. There are a variety of embroidery to choose from, like Rabari embroidery, Bavalia embroidery and Banni embroidery. The state also takes pride in producing gold embroidery that is usually done to enhance the look of fabrics meant for weddings etc.

Dhurries

Most of the villages in Gujarat are famous for weaving some of the finest carpets, blankets and rugs. Woven on the primitive pit looms that is unique to the villages of Kutch these dhurries are in great demand all across the globe. These dhurries involve a lot of hard work as they are made by hand. The carpets and rugs are known for their beautiful designs, colors schemes and intricate weaving.

Jewellery

Gujarat jewelry has been a heritage of India for more than 5,000 years. In early Gujarat, people made jewelry out of natural materials such as seeds, feathers, leaves, berries, fruits, flowers, animal bones, claws and teeth. Even today such jeweleries are used by the tribal people.

Gujarat jewelry is made almost for each and every part of the body. The jewelry in Gujarat ranges from religious to purely aesthetic one. These are made not only for human beings but also for the deities, ceremonial elephants and horses.

Paintings

Paintings in Gujarat are well-known and identified as styles of miniatures, mostly of religious themes. Long after the foundation of the gujarat Sultanate in the 15th century and the establishment of the Mughal rule at the end of the 16th century,paintings in gujarat maintained its angular features as well as its gorgeous and bold colors.

Tangalia

Tangalia is a handicraft which is made solely in Gujarat in the district of Surendranagar. The Dangasia community is the only maker of this peculiar craft.

Tangalia is a sarong like garment worn by the Bharvad women on special occasions such as weddings, or when they visit their relatives. The Ramraj Tangalia is a unique kind of motif worn by Motabhai Bharvad community

Printing and embroidery

Printing and embroidery in Gujarat reveals a cultural tradition that has evolved through centuries.Most of the best and earliest textiles were created in Gujarat. Printing and embroidery in Gujarat has a huge world market.

Varieties of embroidery in Gujarat include:
- Toran, the embroidered doorway decoration with hanging flaps, which is said to ventilate good luck.
- Pachhitpatis, hanged from the corners as a welcome symbol to the visitors.
- Chaklas, used as furniture covers.
- Bhitiya, a wall hanging.
- Abhala, where small mirror discs are fixed with closely worked silken thread.

Woodcraft

Woodcraft in Gujarat exhibits the traditional art of amazingly beautiful wooden handicrafts. These woodcrafts are employed both for utilitarian as well as architectural purposes.

The woodcraft in Gujarat is primarily derived from the wood of the following hardy trees:

* sal
* teak
* sheesham
* deodar
* redwood
* rosewood
* red cedar
* ebony

Music and Dance

Gujarat has contributed several ragas to classical music, marked by territorial names like Bilaval, Sorathi, Khambavati, Ahiri and Lati. Lullaby, Nupital, Rannade songs are varieties of folk songs. Marsias are sung at death. The Vaishnava cult has a particular variety of temple music.

Besides, Gujarat has unique wind instruments like Turi, Bungal, Pava, String type Ravan Hattho, Ektaro, Jantar and percussion instruments like Manjira, Zanz pot drum, etc.

Gujarat music and dance is distinguished by several folk dance forms like:

* Garba-is a popular dance form of Gujarat. It is a circular form of dance performed by women on the Navaratri, Sharad Purnima, Vasant Panchami, Holi and similar other festivals. The word Garba is sourced from 'Garbha Deep', implying a lamp within a perforated earthen pot and indicating new life. In this dance form, ladies place the pot with the lamp on their heads and sway in circles, keeping time by clapping or snapping of fingers, accompanied by folk instruments.

- The actual performance starts at night after the women complete their domestic duties. They assemble at street corners. A photograph of the deity or a lamp is placed centrally and a circle formed about it. Dancing gradually paces up. The rhythm is maintained by a Dholi (drummer).

- During Garba, often, women bear on their heads a small canopy of bamboo chips shrouded with a red silk cloth known as 'Mandavali'. They dance with it and later put it in the center. Mandavali embodies the temple of the goddess.

- Women attire themselves in Gujarati style sarees. Each community wears various clothes. In Saurashtra, women wear embroidered petticoats (Ghaghara), a backless choli (Kapdu) and a head cover (odhani) accessorised by silver and head ornaments. Males wear Kediyum (shirt), Vajani (trouser) and Rumal, a printed head piece with silver ornaments adorning their waist, neck and hands. The instruments accompanying the Garba are the drum (dhol) and Nal.

- Raas-Raas dance, probably originating in Kutch and Suarashtra is currently popular everywhere in Gujarat. The Raas form seems to hail right from the Puranic period. In different parts of India, Raas is danced in different ways. The principal feature of Raas is dancing in a circle by men and women, accompanied by musical instruments and keeping time either by clapping or striking two sticks together. The number of participants may go upto 8,16,32 or even 64 couples, who also sing in chorus. Three forms of Raas are there:

- Danda Rasaka- Raas dance accompanied by danda (sticks)

- Mandala or Tala Rasaka- Raas dance accompanied by clapping.

- Lata Rasaka- Raas dance where dancers hold onto each other and dance like a creeper to a tree.

- Most Gujarati art forms date back to the mythological era of Lord Krishna, supposedly the exponent of this dance form. Raas Nritya was believed to have been performed by lord Krishna with his Gopikas.

- The Dandia variety is usually performed by a group of young boys and girls, swaying in circles to measured steps, beating time with small sticks (called dandia) against a background of songs sung to the Dhol, Cymbals, Zanz, flute or Shehnai. When the beat is kept by clapping and performed only by men, it is called Garbi.
- The Gof variation is an intricate performance in which the performers holding colored strings attached to a top, dance in circles weaving various patterns.
- The Mers of Saurashtra are famous for their folk dance form known as Mer Raas and the shepherds or agriculturists of southern Gujarat dance the Gher or Gheria Raas.
- Raas is a very popular traditional dance form of Gujarat.

SPIRITUAL ARCHITECTURE

Apart from the palaces, forts and castles, Gujarat is blessed with the presence of many spiritual architectures well. The temples, mosque and mausoleums architectures of Gujarat are of the great contributions of the culture. Some of the finest temples of Gujarat were found during the Solanki dynasty.

In the heritage of Gujarat, one can see an influx of Muslim Arabs and Persians. Muslim rulers created gateways, monuments, and multi-storey architectures. Muslim Arabs and Persians have improved the pallet of Gujarat architecture by introducing some concepts like half-doomed portal, domes, stalactites, squinches arches, pendentives, and honeycombing. Other religious communities too had a long term association with Gujarat. During the colonial period, there was a tremendous increase in the number of churches. Even Parsis arrived in Gujarat when they fled from their prosecutor in their homeland in Persia. Historians even say that Guru Nanak has travelled widely in Gujarat when he was embarking on a trip to Mecca via Lakhpat.

Akshardham in Gandhinagar, Sun temple at Modhera, Toran gate at Vadnagar , Shiv Shakti Mandir and Lakha Dera Jain Temple in Vijayanagar, Navlakha temple in Ghumli, Dwarkadhish temple in Dwarka, Jama Masjid in Champaner, Jami Majid in Ahmedabad, Mahabat Maqbara in Junagadh, Sidi Sayyid Mosque in Ahmedabad, European tombs, Badshah no Hajiro in Ahmedabad, Rani no Hajiro (Queen's Tomb) in Ahmedabad, and Gurdwara Lakhpat Sahib in Lakhpat are the most stunning examples of spiritual architecture in Gujarat.

ARCHITECTURE

Architecture or structural design is possibly the outline of human attempt, which furnishes perceptiveness into man's perpetual efforts to achieve perfection, his endeavor to articulate himself, his surroundings, and his stance towards existence, his civilization and his visual sense. Apart from this, architecture is conceivably the only outline which mirrors the development, splendor and riches as well as the retreat, putrefy and paucity of a society, or even a sovereignty or a reign of a certain period.

Gujarat is located at the farthest west of India opposite the Arabian Sea. The most important faith in Gujarat was Jainism and hence the majority segment of the structural designs of this place constitutes Jain temples. It was during the 11th and

13th centuries that the Hindu architecture attained its peak of brilliance as well as artistic radiance and this is manifested by a few of the supreme and most excellent samples of Gujarati designing that prospered during the Solanki as well as Vaghela period. Alas following the invasion from the Muslims, the Hindu as well as Jain temples were shattered and the resources were utilized to build mosques. A few of the notable memorials of Islamic architecture can be found in Ahmedabad in Gujarat. The icon of Islamic architecture is the Mosques in Ahmedabad.

The architecture style which originated in Gujarat while the Muslims ruled was indisputably the loveliest of the regional styles of Mohammedan architecture in the northern as well as western parts of India. It disagreed principally from that developed in northern India, where big and grand structures were raised by the Moguls on a gigantic and wide-ranging scale. Although Gujarat was comfortable with constructions of humble dimensions, they were noticeable by a prominent degree of excellence in their implementation and creative brilliance. The tool of inserting light and air via pierced screen as well as window tracery with venires decorated by a wealthy assortment of geometrical and flowery designs was exclusive. The passive light and assurance in the whole atmosphere, it formed, were promptly pleasant and comforting. Decoration of different parts, towers, structures, balconies and niches was excellent and unmatchable in opulence of facts and creative style. The trembling towers of Ahmedabad are even now the admirations of the world. Fortresses, castles, temples, synagogues, mansions, mosques, sepultures, creative figure of Idols on Stone entrances and step wells which subsist these days in and around Ahmedabad are the bright reminiscences of the expertise and deftness of those who did them.

In fact we can say that Gujarat is spotted with antique Hindu, Jain, Buddhist, and Muslim memorials. The architectural ideas postulated in these memorials mirror the grand legacy of Gujarat arts with culture.

Mahmud Ghazni in 1025-26 A.D sacked the Hindu temples at Somnath and this marked the decisive moment in Gujarati structures. Ghazni's violation and looting of Somnath worked as a catalyst and witnessed Indo-Aryan style architecture in Gujarat attain its peak. This was the period during which authentic and extensive architectural movement in Gujarat took place.

Solanki Dynasty from 1000-1300 AD - One distinctive facet of this era was the expansion of 'Toran' and 'Kirtistambha' architecture.

The noticeable attribute of these Toran and Kirtistambha is an affluent decoration. Whilst Toran functioned as an entry, the Kirtistambha was essentially ornamental, destined to augment the exquisiteness of the overall building. Through the same era temple architecture has arose in Gujarat which is mostly founded on the fundamental thinking on Indian Shilpashastra and Vishwakarma Vastusashtras that itself is founded on 'MANADAP' arrangement (of a covered porch open to all slopes). It has its source in the very antique Vedic age, when non-permanent Mandaps were built for auspicious occasions, marriage ceremonies and Yagnas. With passage of time these Mandaps were prepared as palaces and shrines with gorgeous pillars, engraved roof, ceilings of delicate craftsmanship and striking Toran. The premium instance of temple structural design is the Sun Temple located at Modhera. These were a few examples of wonderful architectural memorials in the nation.

The Indo-Saracenic approach of structural design sprang up during the Islamic rule in Gujarat. Later on the Muslim architecture built Mosques of Honey-colored sandstone which was an unusual and cheerful blend of Muslim and Hindu styles.

The mansolea, mosques and pavilions were the blend of the ascetic principles of Islamic design and the conventional Hindu art of carved decoration. This technique is most extraordinarily presented by the memorials of the significant city of Ahmedabad, which evolved throughout the Muslim phase in Gujarat and was indisputably the most stunning of the regional approach of Mohameden architecture in the western as well as northern India.

The tool of inserting air and light via pierced screen as well as window decoration with panels decorated by a wealthy assortment of geometrical and flowery designs was exclusive. The passive light and assurance in the whole atmosphere, it formed, were promptly pleasant and comforting. Decoration of different parts, towers, structures, domes, balconies and niches was excellent and unmatchable in opulence of facts and creative style. The trembling towers of Ahmedabad, which form the part of Siddi Bashir Mosque, are still the admirations of the world.

Modern Architecture

At present Ahmedabad has a lot of buildings known as some of the best examples of contemporary architecture. It is a truth that contemporary architecture everywhere in India continues to mirror a western prejudice, whereas on the other hand it has been triumphant in foretelling the provincial expression of Indian people, their customs, values as well as philosophy. Le Corbusier, Charles Correa along with Louis Kahn, have really added towards contemporary architecture in Gujarat.

The assorted designs by these 3 architects are evidence of the reality that they could articulate individual social and religious customs and respects via their creations. And these designs were termed as a novel aspect in contemporary architecture, as these aren't an expression of use but of culture.

Louis Kahn with Le Corbusier was the 2 key counselors whose teachings Mr. B.V.Doshi scrambled to fuse their idea in a way to deal with Indian situations. Therefore we can view the viewpoint of the 4 geniuses, but giving individual thoughts of each designer.

Le Corbusier

Le Corbusier made use of adequate amount of bricks and concrete by impregnating them with a tangible sense of space as well as light. His Indian along with spiritual building was the combination of celestial and ancient themes, while his home designs were 'on the cutting edge of peasants'.

Louis Kahn

The natural works of Kahn applied light geometry, structure and a strong concept to tap an ageless aspect, with each novel task he attempted to break in the basic human sense of the institution.

Charles Correa

Charles Correa's fundamental attitude of his buildings was to provide lengthy passageways and extensive arches, which offer shade and aeration. A specimen of his construction styles can be seen at Gandhi Ashram which was designed in 1962. He has productively articulated his viewpoint mixing with regional customs.

B.V. Doshi

Doshi has merged certain permanent values of contemporary architecture with research addicted to the foundation of Indian custom. Doshi has shed light on a terminology of his own by means of vaults sheltered courts, green platforms, water gardens and covered sources of light. Doshi has attempted to determine a reciprocally constructive and inspirational balance between industrialized towns with rural base. Doshi's constructions symbolize a mental picture of man in accord with the nature's order. It is a perfection which blends the reformist attributes of the contemporary movement with a remote and early religious tradition. Doshi also takes into account the fabled and poetic scope of nature, the surge of breeze as well as water, the agreement of light with shade, the association between earth and sky. Doshi did not distinguish between architecture with Urbanism. Individual houses are a theory of an improved kind of city – common space, terrace, rooms, street and court are all connected.

Modern Indian Architecture

Mr. Doshi mentioned to the requirement of constructing building of 'interposed open spaces, courts and terraces'.

Architecture was not only to dish up basic human wants but also provided the structure for communal rituals. Climatic version was to be articulated via the key structure. Buildings were supposed to be thought as collections competent of expansion and change. In addition, there were strong clues about the forms that would best articulate his ideas.

1. The building outline will encompass natural light, movement of air, and access components against the sky to put across the celestial relationship.

2. The base of the building will slowly widen near the floor via steps, platforms, terraces.

3. The building imprint will incorporate rooftop, water bodies, rainwater falls, natural scenes and gardens to hang.

4. The interminable completion of the building will express one homogeneous method yet will have sufficient aspects / compositions / surface balances.

5. The main entry to the building was placed at higher levels with plans for a subordinate entry to convey duality.

6. All the developments inside the building will not be symmetrical but will present astonishing experiences and give double/ambiguous impressions.

7. Artistic contemplations will keep in mind local imagery, contact, and acquaintanceships. Radiating shadows, rhythms in structure, emptiness, solids and banking of marks will be the means of expressions.

FAIRS

A five-day festival is held during Maha Shivaratri at the fort of Girnar, Junagadh, known as the Bhavanth Mahadev Fair. The Kutch Festival or Rann Festival is a festival celebrated at Kutch during Mahashivratri. The *Modhra Dance Festival* is a festival for classical dance, arranged by the Government of Gujarat's *Cultural Department*, to promote tourism in state and to keep traditions and culture alive.

Tarnetar Fair, Tarnetar

The Ambaji Fair is held in the Hindu month of Bhadrapad (around August–September) at Ambaji, during a time which is particularly suitable for farmers, when the busy monsoon season is about to end. The Bhadrapad fair is held at Ambaji which is in the Danta Taluka of Banaskantha district, near the Gujarat-Rajasthan border. The walk from the bus station to the temple is less than one kilometre, under a roofed walkway. Direct buses are available from many places, including Mount Abu (45 km away), Palanpur (65 km away), Ahmedabad and Idar. The Bhadrapad fair is held in the centre of the Ambaji village just outside the temple premises. The village is visited by the largest number of sanghas (pilgrim groups) during the fair. Many of them go there on foot, which is particularly enriching as it happens immediately after the monsoon, when the landscape is rich with greenery, streams are full of sparkling water and the air is fresh. About 1.5 million devotees are known to attend this fair each year from all over the world. Not only Hindus, but some devout Jains and Parsis also attend the functions, whilst some Muslims attend the fair for trade.

The Tarnetar Fair is held during the first week of *Bhadrapad*, (September–October according to Gregorian calendar), and mostly serves as a place to find a suitable bride for tribal people from Gujarat.

The region is believed to be the place where Arjuna took up the difficult task of piercing the eye of a fish, rotating at the end of a pole, by looking at its reflection in the pond water, to marry Draupadi. Other fairs in Gujarat include Dang Durbar, Shamlaji Fair, Chitra Vichitra Fair, Dhrang Fair and Vautha Fair.

The Government of Gujarat has banned alcohol since 1960. Gujarat government collected the *Best State Award* for 'Citizen Security' by IBN7 Diamond States on 24 December 2012.

FAIRS AND FESTIVALS IN GUJARAT

Festivals of Gujarat are as diverse as its physical features; they are vivid, colourful and beautiful. Various types of festivals are celebrated in Gujarat because it is an electric of people. For people of Gujarat, every day is a celebration, approximately 12,365 fairs and festivals are hosted everywhere which makes the state one of its kinds in the world.

Even the movement of the sun or oncoming of harvesting seasons is a matter of celebration for the people of Gujarat. Navaratri, the festival of feminine divinity in the forms of the goddesses Durga, Lakshmi and Saraswati, is the major festival celebrated in Gujarat.

In fact, Navaratri is the longest dance festival in the world. Similarly, International Kite Festival celebrated during Uttarayan, is yet another famous festival celebrated across Gujarat. Raksha Bandhan, Janmashtami, Bhadra Purnima Fair, Urs, Diwali and Holi are the other festivals celebrated in the state.

Every month of the year keeps on buzzing with different fairs celebration. Agriculture, commercial, industrial, Religious, Trade and the list of exhibitions seems endless. Kite festival, Modhera dance festival, Rann Utsav, Bhavnath festival Mahashvratri, and Chitra- Vichitra Fair are some famous fests of Gujarat. In Industrial hubs like Ahmedabad, Surat, Vadodara and Rajkot keeps on buzzing with the many fashion, art, handicrafts, food and commercial fairs.

For those who are looking for adventurous ways to explore Gujarat, it's time to check out Paragliding Festival, Polo Cycle Race and Run The Rann. All these festivals happen to be the coolest and most amazing adventurous festivals celebrated in Gujarat.

Gujarat is home to diversified tribe population. Tribe festivals of Gujarat present an opportunity for the people belonging to different tribes to bond.

Dang Darbar and Chitra Vichitra Fair are some of the tribe festivals celebrated in Gujarat that may be a spark of a traveller's interest to explore the tribal region of Gujarat. Scrumptious delicacies, beautiful ambience, cordial hospitality, excellent craft and friendly people reason enough to attend the tribe festivals of Gujarat.

With lively Television advertisements, Gujarat tourism has managed to attract the attention of travellers from around the world to their festivals. Pay a visit to Gujarat during the festivals and discover the lively side of the state in a different manner.

GET A TASTE OF THE REAL GUJARAT THROUGH ITS MANY FESTIVALS

The cultural vivacity and richness of the state of Gujarat can well be captured through the many festivals of Gujarat. The beauty of the state's age old traditions is showcased most flawlessly through the many festivals celebrated in Gujarat all year round. Almost all the festivals of Gujarat have something unique and special about them. Some of the top-notch ceremonies/rituals of Gujarat that enjoy global fame include dahi handi breaking ceremony, Dhol beating and the very authentic and shimmering garba dance performances. A festival of Gujarat is in fact incomplete without these above mentioned very traditional, signature rituals from the state of Gujarat. Some of the top festivals of Gujarat may be listed as follows-

Navratri

Navratri is a renowned festival of Gujarat celebrated around the months of October/November with immense pomp and grandeur. The fest continues for nine nights and is an invocation of MA Shakti commonly referred to as Mata Rani. Dandiya nights, garba songs, folk music, competitions, exhibitions, free flow of mouthwatering foods, large crowds dressed in their best garbs and fineries and an overall spirit of carnival make Navratri a one-of-a-kind festival in Gujarat.

Rann Utsav

The Rann Utsav has the famed Rann of Kutch as its locale. The Tourism Corporation of Gujarat Limited organizes the

Utsav/fest each year around the months; February-March and the purpose remains to promote tourism in Gujarat's Kutch region. A six day fest held on the Rann makes the barren, deserted Rann come alive with all sorts of exciting sights and sounds. Craft stalls, dance performances, folk music and songs, food stalls etc dot the Utsav ground making the Rann Utsav, a great Mahotsav indeed.

Bhavnath Mahadev Fair

On the occasion of Mahashivratri that falls in the February month, the Bhavnath Mahadev fair is held. The Bhavnath Mahadev temple standing at the base of Girnar hills in Gujarat's Junagadh city serves as the locale for the Bhavnath Mahadev fair.

The fest features numerous colorful events. One of the interesting rituals of the fair is the procession undertaken by the Nanga Sanyasis seated on elephant back and blowing conch shells plus waving flags. The procession commences on the day of Maha Shiv puja and moves towards the fair ground. As per common beliefs, lord Shiva too participates in the Bhavnath Mahadev fair in disguise.

Vautha Mela Fair

Vautha Fair is an important festival of Gujarat celebrated each year at Vautha; the site of confluence of Rivers Vatrak and Sabarmati. The fair is believed to be one of Gujarat's most magnificent fairs. As per mythology, Lord Kartikeya had visited this location once upon a time. The fair continues for about 2-3 days; is held in November on the occasion of Kartik Poornima. Animal trading is one of the most notable activities taking place in the fair.

Modhera Dance Festival

Modhera Dance festival is a world famed cultural show held at the famed Modhera Sun temple in the month of January and third week of the same each year. Various Indian classical dance forms are presented most aesthetically on the occasion of this festival. The temple set up offers the most apt environ for the rendition of the classical dances.

Kite Festival

The kite festival of Gujarat is indeed a sight to behold. Each year on the day of Makar Sankranti; i.e. around January 14th, several colorful and uniquely shaped kites challenge the gravity by soaring high up in the air and dotting the skyline. The festival is also differently referred to as Uttarayan. Kites high up on the air battle with each other and the air around resound to triumphant cries of joy. People don special traditional attires and savor special foods on this day.

Bhadra Purnima Fair

This three-day fair of Bhadra Purnima is held in September each year. The Ambaji temple serves as the venue for this fair. On the purnima day or Bhadrapada full moon day this amazing fair of Gujarat is held.

Madhav Rai Fair

Madhavrai fair also referred to as Madhavpur is celebrated in vicinity to Porbandar to commemorate the divine wedding of Lord Krishna and Devi Rukmini. The fest is held in the Hindu month of Chaitra; i.e. around months March-April.

Tarnetar Fair

Tarnetar Fair is differently referred to as Trinetreshwar Mahadev Fair and calls forth a huge crowd of tribals all gathering at Tarnetar. This fair is an interesting one as match making takes place among the young boys and girls visiting the fair. Thus a tribal boy of Gujarat would visit this fair in hope of meeting his prospective bride. According to folklore Draupadi of epic Mahabharata had selected Arjuna as her husband through a Swayamvara held at this place which was known as pPanchalPradesh in the ancient era. The fairground houses more than 300 stalls selling a plethora of goods, foods etc. folk music and dance shows will make you groove to the amazing beats and rhythm. Cattle shows, embroidery exhibitions, merry-go-round rides, competitive sports are the other attractions of the Tarnetar fair.

Shamlaji Melo

The temple of Shamlaji is located on the banks of River Meshvo and is built completely of white sandstone. The annual fair takes place within the temple premises which is also one of the most sacred pilgrimage centres. The large annual fair which takes place on the eve of Kartik Sud during 15 October, is a huge and magnificent sight to behold. People visit this place to bathe in the holy water and offer their prayers. There are several items which are sold during this fair like silver ware, clothes, Metalware among other household items.

Makar Sankranti

Commonly known as Uttarayan the colorful festival of Makar Sankranti is observed throughout the subcontinent. In the state of Gujarat this festival witnesses a spectacular display of colorful kites in the wide open skies. In the city of Ahmedabad the Patang bazaar comes to life as early as November. On the day of the festival kite flyers gather on the roof and no roof remains empty. The entire atmosphere is encapsulated in regular and pulsating cheers of the people flying these kites.

Rath Yatra

This colorful festival is one of the most awaited annual festivals in Gujarat along with the other parts of the subcontinent. it is majorly celebrated in full enthusiasm in four of the most important places including Jagannath, which is located in Ahmedabad. The main highlight of this festival is a rich cultural procession which is led by an elegant chariot. This grand procession features three separate chariots which are dedicated to Lord Krishna, Balarama and their sister Subhadra.

Janmashtami

Popularly known as 'Krishna Jayanti' this day is celebrated as the birthday of Lord Krishna. His birth is celebrated by decorating Krishna idols and temples with great fun and vigor. People of Gujarat treat this festival as one of the grandest event where all the females treat the idol of Lord Krishna as their own child. Different sweet dishes and Prasadam are prepared with an aim of honoring the almighty lord. Women of the common household observe fasting for the entire day and eat food which has been prepared 2 days in advance.

Chitra Vichitra Mela

This Adivasi fair pursue to all aspects of Indian civilization and culture. This festival kick starts during the eve of new moon when the women of the city gather together by the river and mourn for their dead relatives throughout the night. The entire fair is a generous representation of eclectic colors and dazzling procedures. People douse themselves in their cultural attire complete with a saffron colored turban and Ghaghras while covering them entirely in heavy jewellery. The non stop beating of the drums and the continuous singing of folk songs fill the entire air in deep enthusiasm.

Ravechi Fair

Every year, during the month of September, the stark white salt desert of Kutch comes to life with the oncoming of the famous Ravechi fair. This festival draws a large number of crowds who are on a Hindu pilgrimage and gather from different parts of the world as one. This fair involves color filled cultural dances, folk songs performances and representation of traditional life in Gujarat. Panning for duration of 2 days Ravechi fair showcases a wonderful life of Gujarati locals. There is also an art workshop and exhibition which successfully showcases the core nature of the Gujarati tradition.

Kavant Fair

This tribal festival is celebrated with great pomp and show in mostly the tribal regions of Gujarat. Conducted after the eve of Holi this is a two days event where numerous tourists from in and around the subcontinent visit Gujarat to witness it. This fair is a harvesting festival and during this time people dance in rhythm and celebrate the time with great fun. Numerous artists and musicians flock together as one to this state and showcase their talents here. The performers paint their bodies in attractive colors and unique designs which are made from ash and rice and also create a fun human pyramid.

10

Education

EDUCATION IN GUJARAT

Gujarat is a state situated in the western part of India and shares its northwestern boundary with Pakistan. Rajasthan, Madhya Pradesh and Maharashtra are the neighboring states of Gujarat. Gandhinagar is the capital city of the state and Ahmedabad is its largest city and the main commercial hub of the region. Gujarat houses a wide variety of industries and is considered one among the best industrialized states of the nation. Gujarat is also home to some of the prestigious educational institutes of the nation.

The Gujarat National Law University, Gandhinagar

The education department of the state pays special attention to the improvement of elementary education in Gujarat. The state government has also launched the district primary education program for making primary education compulsory and free for all students up to a certain age limit. It has also taken up several measures for checking the rate of dropout at schools in Gujarat. The same uniform structure of 10+2 education is followed in the schools of Gujarat.

GSHSEB

The Gujarat Secondary and Higher Secondary Education Board (GSHSEB) was constituted in 1972, following the enactment of the Gujarat Secondary Education Act 1972. Its Chairman and Deputy Chairman are appointed by the State Government. It has 16 ex officio members, and 44 other members drawn from academic organizations, legislative bodies and civil society. Various Committees with specific responsibilities function under the Board, such as the Executive Committee, Examination Committee, Finance Committee, Education Committee, and Magazine Advisory Committee.

GSHSEB provides the State Government guidance about the policies governing secondary education, its development and qualitative enhancement. In an overview, its duties are:

- Preparing the curricula & syllabi
- Registering new Secondary schools and monitoring their performance on a continual basis
- Providing developmental guidance
- Organising training for teachers and principals-up measures (for instance, to integrate Gujarat's students with the Information Technology-enabled global village, the Board has introduced Computer Studies among regular curricula).

SCHOOL EDUCATION

Both private and government schools operate here in Gujarat. One can also come across schools run by several municipal corporations and trusts in Ahmedabad.

Gujarat Secondary and Higher Secondary Education Board are in charge of the schools run by the state government. However, many of the private schools in Gujarat are affiliated to the Central Board of Secondary Education (CBSE) and Council for the Indian School Certificate Examination (CISCE) board. Gujarati is the main medium of instruction in the state-run schools while the schools run by other boards use English as their medium of study. The government of Gujarat also gives special importance to education of women in India in the state.

HIGHER EDUCATION

There are several universities functioning in Gujarat which offers both undergraduate and postgraduate programs in various disciplines. The Maharaja Sayajirao University of Baroda is the only English medium university in Gujarat. It was ranked by India Today at the Tenth Place in its list of India's Best Universities (Aug 2011 Issue); while Hindustan Times ranked it at the sixth place. Apart from it, Gujarat University, Saurashtra University, Veer Narmad South Gujarat University, Hemchandracharya North Gujarat University, Bhavnagar University and Kachchh University are the leading State Universities. The four agricultural universities in Gujarat are especially devoted to the study of agriculture and other subjects related to it. Apart from these, Indian Institute of Management Ahmedabad, Sardar Vallabhbhai National Institute of Technology, Surat, Institute of Infrastructure, Technology, Research and Management and National Institute of Design, Ahmedabad are some of the other prestigious centers of higher learning in Gujarat. The state also has some of the best engineering institutes in India like Sardar Vallabhbhai Patel Institute of Technology, Dhirubhai Ambani Institute of Information and Communication Technology among others. Central Salt and Marine Chemicals Research Institute is another reputed institute operating in Gujarat and does various research works on inland lake salt, marine salt and sub-soil brine. In the emerging area of legal education, a premier institution Gujarat National Law University was founded in the capital city Gandhinagar which started imparting education from the year 2004 and is ranked in top institutions in the country.Indian Institute of Public Health Gandhinagar University is the first public health university of india, Launched by Public Health Foundation of India(PHFI), Indian Institute of Public Health Gandhinagar (IIPHG) aims to strengthen the overall health system in the country through education, training, research, and advocacy/policy initiatives.

EDUCATION AND RESEARCH

The Gujarat Secondary and Higher Secondary Education Board (GSHSEB) are in charge of the schools run by the Government of Gujarat. However, most of the private schools in Gujarat are affiliated to the Central Board of Secondary Education (CBSE) and Council for the Indian School Certificate Examinations (CISCE) board. Gujarat has 13 state universities and four agricultural universities.

The premier management college, Indian Institute of Management Ahmedabad ranks the best in India and among the best management universities in the world.

The top-notch institutes for Engineering and Research include IIT Gandhinagar, Institute of Infrastructure Technology research and Management (IITRAM), Dhirubhai Ambani Institute of Information and Communication Technology (DA-

IICT) also in Gandhinagar, Sardar Vallabhbhai National Institute of Technology (SVNIT) and P P Savani University in Surat, Pandit Deendayal Petroleum University (PDPU) in Gandhinagar, Nirma University in Ahmedabad, M.S. University in Vadodara, Marwadi Education Foundation's Group of Institutions (MEFGI) in Rajkot and Birla Vishwakarma Mahavidyalaya (BVM) in Vallabh Vidyanagar (a suburb in Anand district).

The clock tower in Gujarat University, Ahmedabad

Mudra Institute of Communications Ahmedabad(MICA) is one of the most famous institutes for mass communication and is well-renowned across India.

In addition, Institute of Rural Management Anand (IRMA) is one of the leading sectoral institution in rural management. IRMA is a unique institution in the sense that it provides professional education to train managers for rural management. It is the only one of its kind in all Asia.

The National Institute of Design (NID) in Ahmedabad and Gandhinagar is internationally acclaimed as one of the foremost multi-disciplinary institutions in the field of design education and research. Centre for Environmental Planning & Technology University, popularly known as (CEPT) is one of the best planning and architectural school not in India, but across the world; providing various technical and professional courses.

In the emerging area of legal education, a premier institution Gujarat National Law University was founded in the capital city Gandhinagar which started imparting education from the year 2004 and is ranked in top institutions in the country.

Lalbhai Dalpatbhai College of Engineering (LDCE) is also one of the top engineering college of the state.

Kala Bhavan, Maharaja Sayajirao University of Baroda

The Maharaja Sayajirao University of Baroda, Vadodara, is a premier university of Gujarat. It is one of the oldest universities of Gujarat and provides education in Faculty of Fine Arts, Engineering, Arts, Journalism, Education, Law, Social Work, Medicine, Science and Performing Arts. Originally known as the Baroda College of Science (established 1881), it became a university in 1949 after the independence of the country and later renamed after its benefactor Maharaja Sayajirao Gaekwad III, the former ruler of Baroda State.

Gujarat University, Kadi Sarva Vishwavidyalaya, Sardar Patel University, Ahmedabad University, Saurashtra University, Veer Narmad South Gujarat University, Dharmsinh Desai University and Hemchandracharya North Gujarat University are also amongst reputed universities, affiliating many reputed colleges.

Research

The Space Applications Centre (SAC) is an institution for space research and satellite communication in Ahmedabad, India, under the aegis of the Indian Space Research Organisation (ISRO). Dr. Vikram Sarabhai, a renowned scientist, industrialist, and visionary Gujarati, played an important role in it.

He also founded Physical Research Laboratory, a research institute encompasses Astrophysics, Solar System, and cosmic radiation.

He also envisioned Indian Institute of Management Ahmedabad, one of the internationally reputed management research institute that is located in Gujarat's commercial capital Ahmedabad and is the top ranked management institutes in the country.

Central Salt and Marine Chemicals Research Institute has been established under Council of Scientific and Industrial Research Government of India at Bhavnagar. It was inaugurated by Late Pandit Jawaharlal Nehru, the first Prime Minister of India on 10 April 1954, with a view to carry out research on marine salt, and salt from inland lakes and sub-soil brine. It is working on reverse osmosis, electro membrane process, salt and marine chemicals, analytical science, marine biotechnology, and other related fields. The Gujarat National Law University situated at Gandhinagar is the 5th Best Law School currently in India.

Rocket model at Science City, Ahmedabad

Gujarat Science City, is a government initiative to draw more students towards education in science, which hosts India's first IMAX 3D theatre, an energy park, a hall of science, an amphitheatre, and dancing musical fountains amongst others. Institute of Management under Nirma University is constantly ranked amongst the top MBA colleges in India. International Institute of Management and Technical Studies affiliated with Gujarat Knowledge Society, European Association for Distance Learning, Association of Indian Management Schools and Ahmedabad Textile Industry's Research Association has performed globally for its Higher Education Certification courses for working professionals. IIMT STUDIES also launched GET SET GO programme in 2013 in Affiliation with Gujarat Technological University and Gujarat Knowledge Society, Department of Technical Education- Government of Gujarat. B.K. School of Business Management is ranked sixth in financial management. K. S. School of Business Management is also an MBA college in Gujarat University providing a five-year integrated MBA course. Shanti Business School in Ahmedabad is a business school offering post graduate diploma in Management through corporate citizenship initiative.

The Institute of Seismological Research (ISR) was established by the Science and Technology Department, Government of Gujarat, in 2003 and is registered as a Society. ISR campus is at Raisan, Gandhinagar, in a sprawling and picturesque area on the banks of Sabarmati river. Aims and objectives include assigning optimum seismic factors for buildings in different regions and long-term assessment of potential. The ISR is the only institute in India fully dedicated to seismological research and is planned to be developed into a premier international institute in few years time.

SCHOOLS

Al Jamea tus Saifiyah

Al Jamea Tus Saifiyah is an Islamic Arabic Academy situated in the heart of Surat city, India which is a leading theological University for Dawoodi Bohras. It was founded in 1814 by the 43rd Dai Syedna Abdeali Saifuddin [R.A].

A connected academy of the same name started in Karachi, Pakistan in 1983.

H.K.Primary School

The H. K. Primary School is located in Ahmedabad, Gujarat, India. It is named after Harivallabh Kalidas, a prominent citizen and cotton mill owner from Ahmedabad. The school is operated by Ahmedabad Education Society. The school offers education from 1st to 4th grade as approved by state of Gujarat.

Prakash Higher Secondary School

Prakash Higher Secondary School is run by Prakash Trust, a registered public educational trust under the Bombay Public Trust Act, 1956.

The school is situated in the city of Ahmedabad (Gujarat) in India, is co-educational and the medium of instruction is English. The school maintains a very high standard of discipline and quality education, with a concentration on the physical, mental and moral development of its students.

Prakash Higher Secondary School is recognised and affiliated to Central Board of Secondary Education (CBSE) - New Delhi. It prepares students for the All India Secondary School Examination at the end of Class-X and All India Senior Secondary Certificate Examination at the end of Class-XII in Science and Commerce group of subjects.

Bibliography

Alva, Joachim: *Leaders of India,* Bombay, Thacker & Co., Ltd., 1943

Ambedkar, B. R.: *What Congress and Gandhi Have Done to the Untouchables,* Bombay: Thacker & Co., 1945.

Anthony, J. Parel : *Hind Swaraj or Indian Home Rule,* Cambridge University Press, 1925.

Ardley, Bridget.*India.*Englewood Cliffs, N.J.: Silver Burdett Press, 1989.

Atri, Ajit : *Gandhi's View of Legal Justice,* New Delhi, Deep and Deep Pub., 2007.

Barker, Amanda.*India.*Crystal Lake, Ill.: Ribgy Interactive Library, 1996.

Burman, J.J. Roy: *Gujarat Unknown : Hindu-Muslim Syncretism and Humanistic Forays,* Mittal, Delhi, 2005.

Coleman, James S. and Rosberg jr., Carl G.: *Political Parties and National Integration in Tropical Africa,* Berkely, 1964.

Cumming, David.*India.*New York: Bookwright, 1991.

Das, Prodeepta.*Inside India.*New York: F. Watts, 1990.

Dolcini, Donatella.*India in the Islamic Era and Southeast Asia (8th to 19th century).*Austin, Tex.: Raintree Steck-Vaughn, 1997.

Gaur, Sanjay: *Narendra Modi : Change We can Believe In,* Yking Books, Delhi, 2014.

Ghoshal, U. N.: A *History of Indian Political Ideas.* London, 1966.

Gupta, L.C., M.C. Gupta, Anil Sinha and Vinod K. Sharma *Gujarat Earthquake 26 January, 2001,* Indian Institute of Public Administration, Delhi, 2002.

Kalman, Bobbie.*India: The Culture.*Toronto: Crabtree Publishing Co., 1990.

Kamath, M.V. and Kalindi Randeri: *Narendra Modi : The Architect of A Modern State,* Rupa, Delhi, 2009.

Kenneth L.: *Ahmedabad: A Study in Indian Urban History*, Berkeley, University of California Press, 1968.

Maheshwari, Shriram: *Rural Development in India: A Public Policy Approach*, New Delhi, Sage, 1995.

Marino, Andy: *Narendra Modi: A Political Biography*, HarperCollins, Delhi, 2014.

Mathur, Y. B.: *Women's Education in India 1813-1966*, Asia Publishing House, 1973.

Mazumder, Sukhendu : *Politico-Economic Ideas of Mahatma Gandhi : Their Relevance in the Present Day*, New Delhi, Concept Pub., 2004.

Mehta, Nalin and Mona G. Mehta: *Gujarat Beyond Gandhi: Identity, Conflict and Society*, Routledge, Delhi, 2011.

Menon, V. P.: *The Transfer of Power in India*, Bombay, Orient Longman, 1957.

Morris-Jones, W.H.: *The Government and Politics of India*, London, Hutchinson, 1971.

Pandian, Jacob.*The Making of India and Indian Traditions.*Englewood Cliffs, N.J.: Prentice Hall, 1995.

Rao, Ramesh N. and Koenraad Elst: *Gujarat After Godhra: Real Violence Selective Outrage*, Har-anand Publications, Delhi, 2010.

Roy, Ramashray : *Gandhi and Patel : A Study in Contrast*, Delhi, Shipra Pub., 2006.

Shalant, Phyllis.*Look What We've Brought You from India: Crafts, Games, Recipes, Stories, and Other Cultural Activities from Indian Americans.*Parsippany, N.J.: Julian Messner, 1998.

Sharma. Ram Nath : *Gujarat Holocaust : Communalism in the Land of Gandhi*, Shubhi, Delhi, 2002.

Swaminathan, R.: *Gujarat: Perspectives of the Future*, Academic Foundation, Delhi, Delhi, 2008.

Wavell, Archibald: *Wavell: the Viceroy's Journal*, Karachi, Oxford University Press, 1974.

Yasin, Mohammad : *Indian Politics : Processes, Issues and Trends*, New Delhi, Kanishka, 2004.

Index

❑❑❑